"As for me, this you and your family," says the Lord. "My Spirit, who is on you, will not depart from you, and my words that I have put in your mouth will always be on your lips, on the lips of your children and on the lips of their descendants—from this time on and forever," says the Lord.
Isaiah 59:21

Dedicated to my loving wife Lorna.

Copyright © 2014 Author Anthony Egar
All rights reserved.
ISBN-13: 978-1495231803
ISBN-10: 1495231801

www.tonyegar.com

I have just come across your book Tony, and found it an inspirational read. You write clearly, and your message is easily understood.

May God bless you and your wife as you continue in His will to know Him more.

Sue from the U.K

I found your story when I was searching for something to inspire me to seek God further in my life.

It has inspired me to get back into His Word and reminded me not to be impatient with God.

I have never doubted there is a living God but sometimes I have doubted that he really has time for me. Your story really has blessed me and given me the inspiration I so needed. Thank you.

Lucy. New Zealand

Once I started to read your story I could not stop, it so inspired me. It makes me want to read the Bible more. Thank you for your beautiful prayer.

Cathy. USA

How To Be Rich in Faith

by Tony Egar

Tony has always been fascinated by the effect believing has on our lives.

After years of reading books, hearing speakers and going to conferences he has found that the effect was temporary.

His personal belief is that we have a believing switch somewhere within us and if we can get it turned on; everything works, but when it is turned off nothing works.

This is his journey to find that switch and turn it on.

Chapter 1

February 2011

The first thing I noticed, I was waking up happy rather than sad. My experiment had been going for a month.

At the beginning of February 2011, I decided I wanted to change; to be different in three years' time. I wanted to change my life.

Fifty five years old and still failing in the area of believing – that was true motivation. All around me people were changing their circumstances by changing themselves and they were doing this by committing themselves to something they believed in.

They would start a university course, get the proper books, attend the lectures, do tutorials, pass exams, receive guidance and somewhere along that journey they would be transformed into a teacher, dentist, or accountant.

And the whole basis for their transformation was immersing themselves in a university course that would take at least three years to complete.

They could turn their believing switch on and keep it on long enough for a significant change to manifest.
Their cocoon was university; their butterfly experience was their degree.

All I've ever wanted to be in life is a successful Christian and I have spent thirty years hearing and reading the Bible but I have not been transformed. I'm still basically the person I was ten or twenty years ago. Sure I have slowly changed over the years but so have my non-Christian friends. I've grown older and wiser but I haven't been transformed.

So I've decided to devote myself to prayer and the Word [Bible] for three years and keep a journal of my journey.

The New Testament contains 27 books.
I am going to read these books out loud every week.
That is my goal. I know it will not be easy and some weeks will be harder than others.

I am going to the University of Believing.
I am immersing myself in prayer and the Word of God and keeping a record of the results.

Here's the good news, my lovely wife Lorna is joining me on my experiment. We are going on a journey. It will be an interesting three years.

Would you like to know what happened to Lorna? Her non-Christian neighbour rang and asked if Lorna would take her to church this Sunday, which she did. This is a very unusual event for us. Is it a sign of things to come?
We will let you know. See you at the end of March.

Chapter 2

March 2011

I have been a Christian for thirty-two years and very rarely have I seen anyone become a Christian through my influence or my wife Lorna's influence. But last Sunday we were privileged to see our neighbour put up her hand when the pastor gave the congregation an opportunity to dedicate their lives to Christ.

Lorna asked her why she wanted to go to church? Why the change? Our neighbour said something happened to her after having a coffee with Lorna. She went away with faith and hope coming into her heart and she also started praying.

It has been two months since we started reading the New Testament.
Is this a result of putting the words of Jesus into our hearts and lives or is it just a coincidence?
Time will tell.

We have told our newly married daughter what we are doing; she has seen us do similar things before. I think she is mildly amused. When I mentioned that we are doing our readings out loud, she was happy to inform me that most people read the Bible silently and not out loud as we were doing.

I have always read the Bible out loud. It is something that I started thirty two years ago and I find it hard to do it any differently now.

One of my first experiences with reading the Bible happened about three weeks after I became a Christian at twenty three years old. Someone had bought me a Bible and told me to read it because this would strengthen me as a Christian. I was sitting in my flat in Melbourne reading the Bible and drinking a beer.

I had always been a drinker and no-one had told me I couldn't drink because I was a Christian. So there I was drinking my beer and reading the Bible, when slowly I began to notice that I was getting more enjoyment out of the Bible than I was out of the can of beer.

Something happened to me that day because I put the beer down and just kept reading.

Chapter 3

April 2011

When I turned fifty years old I had a mid-life crisis and bought a kayak. I designed a sail for it and every Sunday morning I would get up at 4:30am and go out on Moreton Bay to enjoy God's creation. It was peaceful. The sun came up and I put a fishing line over the side and quietly sailed or paddled my way up and down the bay area.

After about a year of this, I was out there one morning, when the sun was shining, surrounded by great scenery with no one else around. Suddenly, something just left me. The enjoyment was gone and also the desire.

I thought this was very strange until I realised this was God telling me to get out of His creation and into His Church.

I hadn't been going to church at all. I ignored this for about six more Sundays and then gave in and went back to church. This happened about five years ago and as time went by I decided to only go every second week.

I never went kayaking again, the desire never returned.
This week I got convicted again and have started to go every week not every second week.

My wrestle with church attendance began as a youngster. I was raised as a Catholic and my family always attended church. I was bored and when my parents gave me a choice, I took the opportunity – freedom at last.

I played football as a teenager and my team drove up to Crystal Brook, a small town north of Adelaide for a weekend competition. On the drive back to Adelaide, my friend's father offered to give me a lift. He had been drinking all day and veered onto the wrong side of the road and hit a semi-trailer. I was asleep and next thing I know the side of the car had been smashed in. We nearly died that night.

A sense of foreboding came over me; I felt that if I had died that night I would have gone to hell. This was a very real experience and affected me so much that I promised God I would go to church every Sunday, but it didn't last.

About eight years later at the ripe old age of twenty three years I really did dedicate my life to

God and was immediately changed. I went to church regularly for the next twenty seven years. But I guess I just got burnt out and took a break for a while.

Chapter 4

May 2011

I have witnessed to a lot of people over the years but because they never seem to get saved, I have slowly given up telling people about Jesus and my Christian experience.

I have always had a heart for people to get saved. I was changed and helped when I asked Jesus to take over my life, so I think it is a good idea for others to do the same and there is eternity to think about. Heaven and hell are real to me and it makes me shudder.

Last year I was working at one of my customer's homes, who is a very wealthy man. He's so rich that he had a French artist painting gold leaf on the ceilings and cornices of his house.

One day I was working in the same room as the French artist and we began to talk about art and great artists.
I told him that I considered Jesus a great artist because every time he healed a person I considered that a work of art. He said he hadn't thought about it in that way.

Once a year I work at the rich man's house for two days at a time.

The last time I was there it was a terrible atmosphere. He had been diagnosed with cancer and his children were fighting with him over their inheritance. Everyone was shouting and swearing. It was stirring me up.
On my second morning there everyone suddenly disappeared, except for myself and the rich man.

Next minute he calls me up to the kitchen to talk. He was feeling sick and lonely. We both sat down around the kitchen table while he had a cigarette. I turned to him and said that I should pray for him for some peace; this was brave of me because I had offered to pray for him before and he had angrily refused.
This time he said okay.

I warned him that sometimes when I pray I shout. So I shouted at the top of my voice a prayer for peace. After I finished I slumped into my chair, we were both exhausted. In the silence that followed he turned to me and said, "It's good to have faith!" I am sure a transaction happened that day even though I have not seen him again.

A few weeks after that incident, my hairdresser
was talking to me about Steve Irwin's death.
He asked me what I believe happens after we die.
I told him that there is life after death.

He then starts to tell me a story about his
upbringing in Cyprus. He said that if someone had
something against you, they would get some of
your hair and go into the forest to find a tree that
was dying. They would nail your hair to the tree
and they believed that when the tree died you
would die. He used the term 'nailed to the tree.' I
said I knew someone who was nailed to a tree.
This was exciting news for him.
"Who was that?" he said.
"Jesus was nailed to a tree," I said.
"He died so we wouldn't have to die for our sins."
It was not the answer he was expecting to hear.

I have felt God again giving me a nudge about
witnessing. This is okay. I can rise up and start
believing again. That is the easy part; I also felt a
clear impression that I should start praying for the
sick.

In the last two weeks I have prayed for two of my
customers, one had an ulcer from an operation and
the other customer had pain from arthritis.
I told them to ring me up if something happened.

When the lady with arthritic pain rang back, I was really excited, until she told me she wasn't very happy with my work. It's not easy praying for the sick!

But it is easy for my lovely wife Lorna.

Just a few days after I wrote the previous words, Lorna was at a ladies meeting on Tuesday morning. A woman came up to Lorna and asked her for prayer. A week later the lady came bounding up to Lorna and exclaimed that all her pain had gone. She said she never thought the Lord would do that for her! She broke down in tears; she was overwhelmed by the love and kindness of God.

Chapter 5

June 2011

In April 1983 my wife Lorna and I arrived in the town of Katherine in the Northern Territory. We had been married for 6 weeks. I had become a sales agent for a large insurance company.

I was sent to Katherine to sell life insurance to the 3,000 lucky residents of that very small isolated community. The job was really tough and I wasn't doing that well.

About 6 months later my boss and I went down to Adelaide to a life insurance conference, one of the speakers at the conference was an American from Baton Rouge in Louisiana. He got us motivated with his larger than life stories. He said he didn't worry about knocking on people's doors.

He used to arrive to sign up his clients in a helicopter.
I went back to Katherine highly motivated, I believed. Next month I topped the sales results.

However it didn't last. So my boss suggested we get the tapes from the conference and listen to them to get our motivation and believing going again.

We organised a special night to do this and after about half an hour, I heard him snoring!

I have always been fascinated by the effect believing has on our lives. After years of reading books, hearing speakers and going to conferences I have always found that the effect was temporary.

My personal belief is that we have a believing switch somewhere within us and if we can get it turned on everything works, but when it is turned off nothing works.

I know this is a generalization and there are always exceptions.

My great hope is that as I read God's word and pray, my ability to believe will be strengthened.
I also hope to remove doubt in all its forms.
Doubt is death and believing is life.

Chapter 6

July 2011

We have just been smashed! It's nearly five months since Lorna and I started our journey. Our routine fell over and our personal circumstances took a turn for the worse. Nothing serious, but enough to blow us off course. A financial, emotional and relational storm has just belted us. That's life!

It happens to everyone and I bet it happens to everyone who sets out on any sort of self-improvement course.

We left Katherine in 1984 and went to live in Adelaide.

I worked as a sales representative selling commercial chemicals. It was a good job but the pay wasn't great.

I looked around for another job in the same industry and was rewarded for my efforts. My new job was high paying with a brand new company car. My wife thought I was clever; she was going to find out just how clever I was. We were still short of money every week.

The funny thing was we were short of the same amount of money that we tithed to our local church. I thought the Lord wouldn't mind if I stopped tithing so we could balance our budget. It was the day before Christmas, I had been in my new job for three months, and my sales weren't as high as we had planned.

Thank goodness my employment agreement was for a six month trial so I had another three months to turn things around.

Just an hour before I was to leave the office for my Christmas holidays in my brand new company car, my boss said he would like to chat.
"Tony, you are fired, please hand over the keys to the car," he said.
I couldn't believe it; my contract had three months to go before they could legally do that.

Eventually I took them to the Industrial Relations Court and they were charged with unfair dismissal. My court case was successful for one reason. It was written in my contract that I had a six month trial period. They couldn't fire me after three months. The boss of the company had to write me a cheque for damages.
I learnt two lessons; one is to always tithe, the

second lesson was about written agreements, these matter in court and they matter in life.

The biggest change that has happened to me as I read the Bible is the understanding that in amongst all the stories, and all the miracles, and all the personalities, there is one outstanding factor.

The central issue about the words I am reading is that the Bible contains a legal document called the New Agreement.

Luke 22: 20
At the last supper Jesus took the cup, saying *"this cup is the new agreement in my blood, which is poured out for you."*

Suddenly I was seeing legal agreements wherever I looked. Agreements to buy a house, marriage agreements, insurance agreements – they were everywhere.

This was a very topical subject because we had just been through a large flood in Brisbane and the most important document people had was their insurance policy.

In Romans 7, Paul is uncertain, blown about, and indecisive; he wants to be released from his situation and circumstances.

People caught in the Brisbane floods whose insurance policy was unclear about whether they were covered for flood had the same stress. Romans 8 says; *the law of the spirit of life sets us free from the law of sin and death.*

There were two groups in the Brisbane floods, one with insurance policies in which they were completely covered and those with policies that didn't cover them at all. One group was going to have their house fully restored as new. The second group with faulty policies would only get their houses rebuilt by their own effort and their own funds.

The group with good flood policies had access to the wealth and resources of their insurance companies.
The faulty policies brought bad news and were dead words to those who read and heard and understood what they meant.

The message was that you were on your own, your house is destroyed, and it is not going to be rebuilt or renewed or restored by the insurance companies.
When you drive through the suburbs where the floods hit you can tell who had a good policy and who didn't.

Where you find the good insurance policies, you find activity and hope and houses being rebuilt. You see tradesmen, builders, painters; you see lots of people and it looks like a building revival.

But drive down the street where there are property owners with faulty insurance policies, you will find inactivity, despair, anger, frustration, no builders and no progress. It looks depressing and it is.

Romans 8 tells us, *the same Spirit who raised Christ from the dead lives in you and will give life to your mortal body.*

The reason for this is because you have a policy document with God himself that we call the New Agreement.

The price has been paid which is the blood of Jesus; the agreement was initiated at the last supper and then carried out on the cross before the courts of heaven. This makes it a heavenly legal document written down for us in the Bible.

The Holy Spirit raised, rebuilt and restored Jesus and gave Him a brand new glorified body. If the Holy Spirit can do that for Jesus, can't He also do a similar thing for us?

And if it is written that He will give life to our mortal body doesn't that mean that as a Christians, as sons and daughters of the living God, we have a policy document that covers more than flood; doesn't it cover us for every sickness and disease that tries to ravage our house, our body, the temple of the Holy Spirit?

We have a policy that brings good news; it has words that give us life, we have the same builder that rebuilt Jesus after he was ravaged by the flood of judgment that washed across him on the cross and left him dead in a tomb. Raising Jesus from the dead was accomplished by the Holy Spirit.

Well if He lives in us, won't He repair, restore and rebuild us physically, emotionally, financially and spiritually?

Paul's complaint in Romans 7 is that the agreement Moses initiated so many years before was not helping but hindering him.

It was designed to help him live a better life but instead it was adding to his failings.
It wasn't bringing life it was bringing death.
People in Brisbane found that their insurance policies were intended to help them but in the end

they were not designed to help in their particular set of circumstances.

They were protected from fire, storm, theft and accidents but not flooding caused by a rising river. A few simple words changed people's lives and either lifted them up or threw them down. Some will financially never recover. The lucky ones get a second chance in life.

Chapter 7

August   2011

We are just coming out of the storm.
Being in prayer and the word of God really is
changing us, I don't know whether people around
us would notice, but Lorna and I do notice a
change.

We believe in a different way now, we are standing
up in authority in prayer and really taking a stand
against all opposition in the spirit realm.

We have been praying for our children and
expecting new opportunities to open up for them.

In London, the *News of the World* newspaper has
just been shut down because of the phone hacking
scandal. How the tables have turned for this
newspaper.
Over the years it has exposed people in all walks of
life. It has accused many people and probably
destroyed many lives and reputations.

It reminds me of the scripture in Revelation 12:10.
*"For the accuser of our brothers who accuses them
before our God day and night has been hurled
down."*

One of the great struggles we have as Christians is dealing with accusing thoughts.

In John 8:1-11, Jesus had to deal with a situation which called for the death of a woman caught in adultery. Jesus could not defend or deny her actions.
He knew the Law of Moses demanded her punishment and he had a crowd of men demanding action.

His answer was to raise the standard for the accusers so high that all of them were disqualified.

"If anyone of you is without sin, let him be the first to throw a stone at her."
No-one was qualified except Jesus.
And he said *"Neither do I condemn you."*

Those men represented the Law.
Those men were in charge to lead this woman to Jesus. When they had done this; their job was finished. Jesus took over from them and refused to condemn her.

We can reject all accusation from the devil, from people, and from ourselves because none of us qualifies.

When your thoughts or people's words or circumstances organised by the enemy accuse you, don't worry about defending yourself, just use the strategy that Jesus did.

Say *"Who is without sin can cast the first stone."*

In the book of Ezra 1:1, God moved the heart of Cyrus King of Persia to release the Jews to go back to Jerusalem and rebuild the temple.

In Ezra 4:4-6, we see that the Jews have started to build, but their opponents have hired counsellors to work against them. At the beginning of the reign of a new king of Persia these opponents lodged an accusation against the Jews.

In Ezra 4:11-16 they accused the Jews of being a rebellious and wicked city. All these things were true and so the king of Persia wrote back and stopped the Jews from building the temple.

Accusation has the power to stop you doing what you should be doing.

So for many years the Jews were delayed until the Lord raised up two prophets in Ezra 5:1-2. These prophets encouraged the people to get back to work and they started to build the temple.

This time when they were opposed they refused to stop. Once again their enemies sent a report back to the King of Persia.

But this time things were different, not only was there a new king in Persia, there was also a different search made. [Ezra 5:17]
Instead of focusing on their history, bad behaviour and mistakes of the past, this time they searched the royal archives of Babylon to see if King Cyrus the original King did in fact, issue a decree to rebuild the temple of Jerusalem.

In Ezra 6:1-5 they did find the original decree that did officially authorise the building of the temple.

Our enemies will accuse us all day long to try and delay God's work of restoration that is going on in our lives but we are not subject to our past history, we are subject to God's gifts and His calling.

Romans 11:29 *For God's gifts and His call are unchangeable.*

It's funny that I am writing about God's gifts and his calling because I have been out of ministry for over 15 years. Will God restore me to ministry of some sort? I would be happy to continue on as I am.

The story in Ezra can be summed up like this.

It is a story of two reports, a bad report and a good report.

This reminds us of the problem Moses had when he sent spies into the land and they brought back a bad report in Numbers 13:32.

Meanwhile Joshua and Caleb brought a good report.
Where there is a good report, there is often a bad report. It is incredibly important to ignore the bad report.

In Mark 5: 35-43 Jesus is going with Jairus to heal his daughter.

As they were on the way some men came and told Jairus that his daughter had died. Jesus ignored what they said and told Jairus, "Don't be afraid, just believe."

At this point Jairus had a good report and a bad report and had to choose which one to believe and which one to ignore. Jairus made the right choice and believed the good report and his daughter was raised from the dead.

Chapter 8

September 2011

It's been seven months since I started this experiment and now I have kicked up to a new level.

I don't know why I have increased my effort, it is one of the changes that has happened since I started my course. My church attendance has increased from every fortnight to every week. I have started again giving offerings on a regular basis.

My business has increased. My relationships inside the family were always very good. My relationships outside my own family have been tested and shaken; I think there is more sincerity and truth.

I would like to give you an overview of my church life.

I got saved when I was 23 years old in Melbourne and went to a church called Life Ministry Centre. I stayed there for about three years in which time I spent two years full-time in their bible college.

I met my wife Lorna at that college. We got married and left Melbourne for a small town called Katherine in the Northern Territory.

In Katherine we went to the Anglican Church for 12 months, after this we returned to my home town Adelaide and joined the Assemblies of God Church in the suburb of O'Halloran Hill.

We stayed at this church for about ten years, we served as home group leaders, elders and as pastors, none of these positions were full-time.

Then the local church sent us out to plant a church in Mildura, Victoria. We stayed in Mildura for about three years, but the church plant did not work and we left for Brisbane in Queensland. My family and I have spent most of the last fifteen years at a church called Northside Christian Family Church, which is an Assemblies of God Church.

The Assemblies of God have since changed their name to Australian Christian Churches and the church itself has changed its name to Nexus Church.

These fifteen years at Nexus Church have been very good for my family. My daughter Jessica met and married her husband there, my wife Lorna has found great expression in the ladies ministry, in worship and also in the School of the Supernatural, a course on signs and wonders and praying for the sick.

My son has found expression through the church worship as a drummer and now as a guitarist. And what a contrast, I have done absolutely nothing for fifteen years and have not been moved or motivated internally or externally, by myself or by God.

A few weeks ago I was sitting in church when it was announced that they were not going to have an early morning service through summer. So when I got home that morning I looked up the service times of the churches in our area and found a church that had an 8am Sunday service. I asked my wife if she would mind if I visited a different church next Sunday and she said that was fine!

For the last five weeks I have been going to a church called C3 church in Bridgeman Downs.

The strangest thing has happened, for the first time in fifteen years, I have felt God moving on me as I have been sitting in the church service.
Don't get me wrong, I have felt God in my life, but not recently in my church life and now after fifteen

years of lying dormant I am feeling God move on me as I sit in church.

My wife finds it interesting; some of my friends are slightly alarmed that I am going to a different church than my family. I just tell them that I am visiting and where my family is, my home church is. I have also told the people I have met at this church what my situation is; and so far everyone has found this to be acceptable.

Chapter 9

October 2011

A few days ago I was reading the book of Corinthians and this scripture sure had life on it.

2 Corinthians 4:13

"I believed therefore I have spoken.
With the same spirit of faith we also believe and
therefore speak."

I really felt moved to speak out in authority in my prayer time. I started commanding mountains to move, such as the mountain of debt, the mountain of sickness etc. I also started commanding oppression to go, the powers of darkness to flee.

On top of that I began to declare blessing over my family. I became vocally active instead of being passive. I took up my authority in Jesus name.

I had become pretty relaxed over the years, and in fact I basically stopped believing in this activity of speaking to situations and commanding them to move.

Suddenly I woke up because the scripture says, "We also believe and therefore speak!"

Wow!

If we believe, we speak, if we don't believe we don't speak.

Years ago in the Assemblies of God church at O'Halloran Hill in Adelaide, I ran the new Christians class.

We were an interesting group. One person was an old soldier from the Malaysian insurgency, he had married a Malaysian woman and was living near our church.

I used to pick him up and take him to the new Christians class. I didn't know whether he was saved. One of the lessons was based on Romans 10:9-10.
"That if you confess with your mouth "Jesus is Lord" and believe in your heart that God raised him from the dead, you will be saved."

I got everyone to pray together out loud.
"Jesus I believe you are Lord and that you were raised from the dead."

On the way home I was talking to this old soldier about the class.

He said "Tony when I prayed that prayer out loud something happened in my heart, I could feel God."
This had never happened to him before and he had been unsure about his Christianity, but he believed and he spoke and something good happened.

When we got the opportunity to plant a new church in Mildura we had to get ready quickly.

One problem I had was selling my business, I tried to sell it through a broker and that didn't work.

Two business men thought about buying it but changed their minds. I advertised through the paper and had someone get really interested, but nothing happened.

After all this effort and with time running out, suddenly I got this scripture.

2 Kings 3:17 *"You will see neither wind nor rain, yet this valley will be filled with water."*

What this said to me was "You can't see a buyer but it will be sold." I think a gift of faith dropped into my heart. I had a confidence that was not supported by facts.

Seven days before we were to leave Adelaide I was doing some work in an office building and started a conversation with a man I had never met before.

I told him my story and he said he might be interested in buying part of the business. On Monday he spoke to his bank manager and came to my house to look at the books. On Tuesday he came back and wanted more information.
On Wednesday the bank manager suggested he buy the whole business. On Thursday we agreed on a price! At 5pm Friday afternoon he rang and said it was a deal. On Saturday morning we left for Mildura. Amen.

While we were in Mildura, one of the ministers in Adelaide said he would like to come for a weekend and preach a series of meetings.

I was a bit embarrassed because the numbers were down and it wasn't easy to get everyone motivated, including me. I was thinking to myself, "When he comes what will he find?"
Leading up to this important weekend I was reading the book of Luke chapter 18:8 and this verse jumped out of the page.

"However when the son of man comes will he find faith on the earth?"

I applied this verse to my situation and asked, when the minister comes up from Adelaide, will he find faith?

Bang, another gift of faith dropped into my heart.

I told my wife Lorna, it doesn't matter how many people we have. What matters is that we have faith! And we did have the faith that came through that verse.

We had a great weekend, the numbers were up and the power of God manifested. The minister enjoyed himself and loved the atmosphere of faith. One of his highlights was the Sunday night meeting.

A Salvation Army man came to the meeting in his uniform and when he was prayed for he had a real encounter with the power of God.

These are moments of faith and when they happen it is great.

Having a lifestyle interspersed with moments of faith is wonderful. I know what it is like to have moments of faith. I need to experience what it would be like to be changed into a man of faith.

Chapter 10

November 2011

We have just come back from a week's holiday at Coolum on the Sunshine Coast. The month of November has been quite productive.

A few weeks ago our neighbour Sue was standing next to Lorna at the Sunday evening service. Suddenly the pain in her jaw disappeared. Sue had been having a problem with her jaw and now the pain was gone.

Lorna was recently shopping at the local supermarket when she saw one of the staff members limping, she asked if she could pray for her and the lady said yes. So Lorna laid hands on her ankle and all the pain left. What a thrill!

Yesterday Lorna was at another shopping centre. She noticed a young lady sitting on a chair with a pair of crutches and a leg brace.
Lorna introduced herself and asked if she could pray for the young lady. When Lorna laid her hands on the young lady's ankle, all the pain disappeared.

The young lady was amazed. She was so relieved to not be in pain.

These experiences are fairly new for Lorna and myself. Over the last thirty years most of our prayers for healing have not been a success.

Recently Lorna was suffering from a virus. I had been praying for her with no relief, this had been going on for a few days.

On the third day I was reading Luke 7:6-10. I found a lot of life on verse 8.

"For I myself am a man under authority, with soldiers under me. I tell this one to "go" and he goes and that one to "come" and he comes. I say to my servant, "do this," and he does it."

After reading this I said to Lorna, "If I asked you to make me a cup of tea would you do it?"

She said "yes".

So I said, " I am asking you to be healed of this virus."

As soon as I said these words she was healed, the virus left! Pretty amazing!

Years ago when I was a young pastor in Adelaide, I was asked by the church leaders to start up a healing team so we could pray for the sick at the church meetings and also for sick people that we knew outside the church.

A lot of the people we prayed for died. Most of them had cancer and this was beyond our experience and faith. Lorna and I have always had a heart for the sick.

We would love to see a lot of healings. This is a common attitude for most Christians, so we are not alone.

I wonder if the healings we have seen in the last few weeks are the beginning of something new! Mark 4: 28 [NKJ] says, "First the blade, then the head, after that the full grain in the head."

Another theme that is occurring in the month of November is the theme of sowing and reaping. Luke 8:11 says, "The seed is the word of God."

I have heard a lot about this theme in sermons and books since I have been a Christian.

Years ago a Christian magazine had a story about a man who had been cured of cancer by reading out loud a list of healing scriptures. I thought this was a great story. The list of scriptures was printed in the magazine.

I got these scriptures and spoke them out loud for a long time, but nothing happened. One of the lessons I learnt was, we can't cause a miracle of healing to happen by using a formula.
Obviously God had told that man to read those scriptures, and he was healed because the instruction came from heaven.

The two sons of Abraham have a similar story. Ishmael was born because of a man's idea and Isaac was born because the idea came from heaven.

Matthew 4:4 says, "Man does not live by bread alone, but by every word that comes from the mouth of God."

There is nothing better than to get a fresh word of faith from heaven. We may be surrounded by a thousand good ideas. And then light and insight breaks through from heaven.

Jesus kept on saying "Repent, for the kingdom of heaven is near." Does this mean that a word from God is never far away?

As I continue to read the Bible I am reading with a different attitude. I am reading with expectation in my heart.

In 1 Samuel chapter 3, the boy Samuel ministered before the LORD under Eli. In those days the word of the LORD was rare; there were not many visions.

This passage of scripture tells the story of a young boy who had not yet discerned the voice of heaven.

The older man who was his guardian had to teach him to expect to hear from God. It was a period of time when the word of the Lord was not heard very often.
But that was about to change.

Samuel became a great prophet and was known as a person who heard from God. As I read the New Testament it can be mechanical and repetitive.

So I have to keep remembering that it is a living word.

Just as every day is the same but every sunset is different. I am being trained to keep my heart open towards heaven as I read the Bible. I have to repent and remember that the kingdom of heaven is near.

The two ladies Lorna prayed for had been going about their daily lives and along comes Lorna with a touch of heaven on her life. She laid her hands on these women and the pain left them. This is a great illustration of how near heaven can be.

Chapter 11

December 2011

Yesterday was Christmas Day. It was a great day. We went to my daughter Jessica's house. It was the first time one of our children hosted Christmas Day.

My experiment has been going on for ten months.

It is the time of year when we all cross over into a new season. I feel that I am crossing over in my faith. My eyes continually look at my circumstances for proof that being in prayer and the Word is working.

Lately I have been able to take my gaze from what is seen and fix my eyes on what is not seen, the invisible realm. It is not my natural eyes that see the invisible realm. It is the eyes of my heart.

I believe that my circumstances are changing even though I cannot see them physically changing as quickly as I want. My thinking and believing are also changing.

In the past I would read the Bible and receive a word of faith. Over the last thirty years I have received many words of faith, some wonderful and encouraging words. These words have been fairly unpredictable. They have been God's gift to me at different times and in different ways.

Now as I read the Bible I believe every word has the breath of God on it and in it. I have realized that I don't read for the sake of knowledge. I read because I am thirsty and hungry. Hungry for spiritual life. I am only satisfied these days by words of formation instead of words containing information.

Adam and Eve chose the tree of knowledge. There was another tree in the garden called the tree of life! This explains what has happened to me lately.

I have chosen life!

It appears my mind is being fed, but what is really happening is that I am eating and drinking spiritual words for their spiritual life by the Holy Spirit into my spirit. My mind has become a little stronger because it has received a little more knowledge. My spirit is where the growth has been. My spirit can perceive spiritual truth far easier now.

That is why I can believe even though my circumstances appear unchanged or little changed. My favourite scripture at the moment is:

Romans 8:2

"The law of the spirit of life set me free from the law of sin and death."

This thought that life is stronger than death has been planted in my mind and into my heart. Because I am reading these words that contain life I have begun to expect that everything that represents death will start breaking from my situation.

My world can be split into two headings. Things that are good for me manifest out of life and things that oppose me have death behind them.

So I can put debt and sickness in the death column.

Here is another favourite scripture.

Romans 8.11

"And if the spirit of him who raised Jesus from the dead is living in you, he who raised Christ from the dead will also give life to your mortal body through the spirit, who lives in us."

I must be better off if there is more of God's life around me and in me. So reading God's Word and

praying must be a good idea.
I have always struggled to maintain positive speech while in a negative situation.

My work takes me into retirement villages every week. In fact I have been surrounded by the elderly for over 20 years. There is a speech pattern that the elderly share and it's not often a positive one.

Their bodies and minds are slowly being overtaken by the ravages of old age. So most of their observations are based on facts.

Sarah and Abraham had the same problem.
In Romans 4:19-21 Abraham faced the fact that his body was as good as dead, since he was about 100 years old.

Some of my customers are between eighty and one hundred years old. For over twenty years I have been watching people age and die. This has affected my own thinking and speech patterns.

Abraham and Sarah received a renewing of their bodies. God enabled them to have a son, when it was physically impossible. Something has happened to me lately because I find that I am no longer influenced by an older person's mindset.

I have been given the ability to believe for my health and my life to get fitter and better as I get older. Before this, everything was about growing old gracefully.

But now my focus has changed from death to life, my expectation has changed and so has my speech.

I am believing for God to miraculously uphold Lorna and myself in all our circumstances.
Psalm 103:5 says," God satisfies our desires with good things so that our youth is renewed like the eagles".

Old age really had gained the upper hand. Now the life of God has gained the upper hand. All our battles are lost or won in our heart and in our believing.

This was a battle that I was always losing. This is a battle that I am now winning.

The law of the spirit of life has set me free.

Chapter 12

January 2012

I have just finished 12 months of reading the Bible and praying. From the beginning I have thought of what I am doing as a 3 year university course.

I watched my daughter Jessica do a three year course at university. How did she feel at the end of year one? Greatly relieved to finish the first year.

A popular program on television at the moment is called *Grand Designs*.

I find it fascinating to watch these people put themselves through trials and tribulations when they build their houses. Every time they build they go through four different phases.

Phase one; they do all the foundations, phase two; they build the house until it is watertight.
Phase three; they fill the house with all the fittings and furnishings and phase four; they invite the television crew back to show the completed house.

Proverbs 24:4 *By wisdom a house is built, through understanding it is established, through knowledge its rooms are filled with rare and beautiful treasures.*

In most of the stories, these people have been changed by their experience.

By completing my first twelve months I have also been changed. I wouldn't say it was a big change but it has been foundational.

My church attendance has improved. My offerings have become regular. My relationships have been shaken, most have survived.
My health has also improved.
I have met more people in the wider church.
My finances are better organised. My wife says I have become a better person. My work ethic has increased.

My believing has certainly changed for the better. I do have more faith. Last year was a digging out of foundations. This year I expect walls to go up, a roof to be put on, windows and doors to be fitted and hopefully by the end of the next twelve months in January 2013.
I will be watertight, no leaks, and no doubts.

In the past, when I have done this sort of thing, I would not finish my course and so I would be double-minded. Not this time, I have really run this part of the race.

1 Cor 9:25. *Everyone who competes in the games goes into strict training.*

One of the themes that keeps coming to my mind when I read the New Testament is the theme of the Cross of Christ.

This is not surprising because the New Testament is all about the death and resurrection of Jesus. I keep getting the urge to go into Brisbane on a Saturday night and walk around with a wooden cross on my back.

The family are quite relieved that I haven't done this yet. By reading the Bible as I have, the story of the crucifixion has been impressed onto my thoughts and imagination.

One of the areas I have always struggled with is debt. Before I was a Christian I had no debt. In 1979 I got saved and in 1980 I went to Bible College full-time.

I had saved up for this first year of college but I didn't have any money for the second year. My grandfather died that year and left me his piano. I didn't play piano. I am not musical. My family have always been perplexed about why my grandfather gave it to me.

I sold the piano for $4,000 dollars and paid for my second year of Bible College. I had about $800 left after my fees. This money would have been enough to keep me for the rest of the year.

One day we went into lectures and the pastor told a story about being in America on a ministry trip and he gave away every dollar he had and trusted God. I was young and easily influenced so I gave away my $800 dollars and trusted God.

From that day till now I have never had enough money and have relied on debt. A few hours ago I said to my wife, "Do you realize I had no debt before I was a Christian?"

Talk about digging out your foundations, I was digging down to the rock.

My wife and I prayed about that decision I had made 30 years ago. It sure sounded right at the time. Looking back from where we are now, the path we took was the wrong one. I shouldn't give away money if it's going to make us dependant on debt.

Do you like this scripture? I do.

1 Thessalonians 4:11-12

Make it your ambition to lead a quiet life, to mind your own business and to work with your hands just as we told you, so that your daily life may win the respect of outsiders and so that you will not be dependent on anyone.

Chapter 13

February 2012

I have taken a break from reading the New Testament and for the last month I have read the Old Testament. I split it into four parts and have taken a week to read each part.

Genesis to Ruth, 1 Samuel to Esther, Job to Isaiah, Jeremiah to Malachi.

If you are at university and you have completed your first year of study, when you go back for the second year you don't expect to be at the same level as you were when you started.

You say to yourself, "I have completed year one, now I am going to a new level, my second year." Because I know what I have done, I also expect to go to a new level in my second year. If doubts or arguments come against me I just refute them with logic. I have done it. It is finished. I am moving on.

I act like a second year student. In your second year at university you are bolder and more confident. You know your way around. You carry more authority, now you are telling first year students where to go and what to do.

A few months ago my son Samuel asked me to go with him to a large shopping mall. He said "Dad, I want to buy you a new set of clothes because I believe you are going to a new level in life!" Thank you Samuel!

At church recently the pastor said prosperity means going to a new level, his words had real life on them.

Here is a letter my son-in-law sent me.

Tony, I was reading the gospel of Luke last night and I believe God gave me a word for you.

Luke 18:27-39
He replied, "What is impossible for people is possible for God."
Peter said, "We've left our homes to follow you."
"Yes," Jesus replied, and I assure you that everyone who has given up house or wife or brothers or parents or children, for the sake of the kingdom of God, will be repaid many times over in this life, and will have eternal life in the world to come."

I know that you have given up much in your life to follow after God's purpose and will, and you have had to sacrifice relationships, friendships, money, time and opportunity for the sake of God's kingdom and purpose.

I believe that God will repay you for the faithfulness that you have shown him and that impossibilities will become possible.

You have risked much for the kingdom but there is much to be returned to you.

Your family, myself included, is incredibly proud and inspired by you and Lorna for the relentless faith that you have demonstrated throughout your life.

That is a great letter. It is an encouragement. Thank you Joshua.

Here is a key to help you hold on to your new level. Don't fix your eyes on what you can see. You may see some great results. If you put your confidence in those results you are building on sand. You may get a promotion at work but that promotion may disappear. Then what are you going to believe?

Mark 11:24
"Whatever you ask for in prayer believe that you have received it, and it will be yours."

I believe my faith has increased not because of my circumstances. It has increased because the amount of God's word has increased in my life.

How could I be worse off? I have read the New Testament every week for a year.

I must be in a better place than when I started; especially if you allow the word of God to work in you. It has gone down into my spirit. It has strengthened and encouraged my spirit.

Ephesians 5:26
To make her (the church) holy cleansing her by the washing with water through the word.

I have been washing myself through the cleansing word of God.

Acts 20:32
Now I commit you to God and to the word of his grace, which can build you up and give you an inheritance.

I have been built up by the word of God and I want my inheritance in every area of my life and the lives of my wife and children and their loved ones.

John 8:32
Then you will know the truth and the truth will set you free!

John 17:17
Your word is truth.

I have spent a year in the truth of God; there must be a change for the better. The bible exposes the lies and distortions that oppose us. Do I sound a bit cranky? You just cannot afford to be passive.

1 Corinthians 9:24-25
Do you not know that in a race all the runners run, but only one gets the prize? Everyone who competes in the games goes into strict training.

Right now across Australia people are training for the Olympics. They believe to go to the next level. They don't believe they are going backwards.

When I completed my first year, I did look to my circumstances for confirmation. I then realized that I had to believe before I could receive it.

So I decided to give myself a promotion of faith. I said to Lorna, "I have gone to a new level of faith."

I believed what I said was true. I could prove it.

James 2:18
Show me your faith without deeds and I will show you my faith by what I do.

I have shown my faith by what I have done. If someone says to me "You haven't changed much,

you look the same to me."
I just say to them "my faith is invisible but my actions are visible, judge me by what I have done."

If someone comes up to me and declares they are in their second year of university, I believe them. And I also believe they would be at a better level now than when they began university.

Here's the good news; you don't have to do what I have been doing. What you have to do is believe that every time you read the Bible you are gaining ground. Even if you are only reading the Bible a little at a time, you should believe that you are being washed and cleansed. You are being built up, you are being strengthened.
A little of the Bible can go a long way.

It depends on what and how you believe. Most people will never do what I am doing. But they can believe what I believe. Every time you read the Bible you do go to a new level.

When I was in Mildura all those years ago we went through a lot of different phases until we closed the church because it really wasn't going to work. During this period I felt an urge to spend a lot of time praying in tongues.

Paul said in 1 Corinthians 14:18 *"I thank God that I speak in tongues more than all of you."*

After about three months a series of circumstances came about that enabled us to conduct some meetings on Sunday nights.

The emphasis was on evangelism and we had a great response. A few of our friends came along and supported us.

As we were leaving our house to go to the first meeting, we were in our car and about to reverse out of the driveway. We heard the phone ringing from inside the house. Lorna jumped out of the car and got to the phone in time.

The lady on the phone was ringing to enquire about the meeting and asked who we were. She had seen our advertisement in the paper.

Because of that phone call, the lady turned up to the meeting and she said she could see the glory of God on me as I preached. This lady was a centre of influence in the local area and she told a lot of people to come to our meetings.

There was a real sense of the Holy Spirit resting on the worship and the teaching of the word. When the meetings became successful I stopped speaking in tongues, I thought it wasn't necessary.

The times of refreshing lasted about 8 weeks. Then the life slowly lifted off what we were doing. At the time I really didn't know what part my prayer life played in those two months.

But I have always remembered that time of blessing and wondered what could have happened? Recently the urge to speak and pray in tongues has returned.

Romans 8:26
In the same way the Spirit helps us in our weakness. We do not know what we ought to pray for, but the Spirit himself intercedes for us with groans that words cannot express.

I have always found that when you are in a small confined place and you want to move to a larger place, the Holy Spirit will pray through you and for you.

Job 36:16
He is wooing you from the jaws of distress to a spacious place free from restriction, to the comfort of your table laden with choice food.

So why do I feel to pray in the Holy Spirit at this particular time? At the beginning of February 2012 the church I go to, announced a month of prayer and fasting.

When Lorna came home from church she also felt to do something in that area. We both decided to fast television for the month of February.

That is no big deal! We have no children at home and now we have got rid of the television. An opportunity to pray has surfaced. More prayer can mean more anointing which can mean more happenings.

I would love to go to a new level of signs, wonders and miracles because the old level was basically near zero. It always helps to start from a low base because any improvement looks good!

Chapter 14

March   2012

I have started my second year of reading the New Testament every week. When people ask me how much time should they spend reading the Bible, I just tell them to read enough of the Bible to keep doubt out.

Don't do it reluctantly or under compulsion because God loves a cheerful reader. When you have read the Bible for thirty years you can afford to be a bit more intense.

I mentioned in February that a season of prayer had descended on our lives. This is still happening. We have the time and none of our children are living at home.

In 1985 Lorna and I had an opportunity to go to Seoul, Korea to visit the largest church in the world for a church growth conference. When we were at the conference Pastor Cho took the delegates up to a place called Prayer Mountain. It was close to the border between North and South Korea.

His church had built a prayer chapel. The main auditorium of the prayer chapel seated ten thousand people. Because our conference group was only about two thousand people they took us into a side room that could seat up to three thousand. The church we were going to in Adelaide had about two hundred people. All of us were impressed with how large everything was. Korea is well known for the prayer life of its churches.

Apparently this started as a prayer revival in a missionary conference held over one hundred years ago. Pastor Cho and his church are great believers in prayer. They think Western people are lazy.

So here we were at a conference on church growth, seated on the floor of a side room at the prayer chapel on Prayer Mountain near the North Korean border.

His specialty at the time was to use the prayer pattern that Jesus taught in Matthew 6:9-13.

Our Father in heaven, Hallowed be your name, Your kingdom come,
Your will be done on earth as it is in heaven.
Give us today our daily bread, forgive us our debts as we have forgiven our debtors and lead us not into temptation, but deliver us from the evil one.

For yours is the kingdom and the power and the glory forever and ever amen.

Pastor Cho taught us to use each verse as a launching pad for different topics and themes. After he taught us he said "You are lazy westerners, you must now pray for one and a half hours!"

We all started praying out loud together and after one hour we were all finding it a bit hard. While all this was happening around me I suddenly sensed that I had a breakthrough. I somehow knew that I had just been given the ability to pray for as long as I wanted. Up to that time I had found prayer to be hard work. But from that moment on I have been able to cross into a realm of prayer that I never knew existed.

You can imagine that from 1985 until now, there have been seasons of prayer that have come upon my life.

When you get asked to preach or teach, you like to spend time in prayer to ask God for help and for His anointing. These occasions of prayer have a purpose; they are not only for you, they are for the people you are going to minister to.

Sometimes when you are praying you sense that heaven has opened and something in the spirit realm has been deposited into your spirit. If this happens to you this is a wonderful experience.

The people you minister to will sense that you have been in prayer and they will see that you have received something from heaven. Everyone gets excited when a blessing drops down from heaven. You feel that you have crossed to the other side, where provision is unlimited.

James 1:17
Every good and perfect gift is from above, coming down from the Father of the heavenly lights, who does not change like shifting shadows.

I had another similar experience to the one I had in Korea. This also happened around 1985. Lorna and I were at a small church in Adelaide. We had been given the job of running a weekly home group. This operates like a small Bible study group. My problem was, even though I could preach, I couldn't teach. I would get to the home group and open up the Bible study and to my horror my words wouldn't make sense. I would muddle through. It was embarrassing.

I had been praying and asking God for help. One day, as I was sitting in our backyard trying to find something in the Bible to share at our home group, I felt something drop into my spirit and immediately I knew it was the gift of teaching. I told Lorna "a gift of teaching just dropped into my spirit!"

At the home group that week I was able to open up the Word in an amazing way. Some of the people came up to me after and asked "Where did you get that from? It was stunning!"

It was stunning and it has remained that way until this day. I can open the Bible at any page and start teaching. It is a gift that I didn't have and I knew I didn't have it. Then I knew I did have it!   Pretty amazing!

Proverbs 18:16
A gift opens the way for the giver and ushers him into the presence of the great.

One of the gifts I have wanted is the ability to see people saved.

Matthew 4:19
Come follow me, Jesus said and I will make you fishers of men!

Most Bible scholars would agree that the ministry of Jesus may have lasted for three years. If we accept this as a general estimate it means that the disciples were taught and trained by Jesus for that amount of time.

I have said before that it takes three years to change a person. Our university courses usually take three years or longer. A lot of what Jesus said and did is written down in the gospels. The book of Acts gives us even more understanding of what the disciples were like after Jesus was finished with them.

One of the things that we would all agree on is that these men really did become fishers of men. Peter on the day of Pentecost cast out his net and caught about 3,000 people.

Acts 2:41
Those who accepted his message were baptized and about 3,000 were added to their number that day.

When Jesus met Peter he had the ability to catch fish. After three years of living with Jesus and being exposed to his teaching and training, Peter had a new ability to catch men.

Luke 5:10
Don't be afraid; from now on you will catch men.

If I spend three years reading the New Testament won't I be exposed to the teaching and training of Jesus?

Couldn't I expect that somewhere along this journey I will find that I have become a fisher of men? If this happens it will be an easy thing to see. It will be a radical transformation.

Romans 12:2
But be transformed by the renewing of your mind.

The word of God is renewing my mind, soul, and spirit.

Last year I was reading Matthew 13:47 "Once again, the kingdom of heaven is like a net that was let down into the lake and caught all kinds of fish." I told Lorna that this scripture had life on it.

The next day our new neighbour knocked on our front door to introduce herself and apologise for her chickens being in our garden.
One thing led to another and five minutes later she accepted Jesus as her personal Saviour.

Lorna had to help her to her car because the power of God came upon her and she didn't know what was going on. Fishers of men have nets and this lady sure got caught in that net.

Chapter 15

April 2012

Last Sunday morning was Easter Sunday. We had communion at church and while I was having communion I thought I would draw a line in the sand and forgive everyone for everything in my past and use Easter Sunday to declare that anything that had happened before that day was dealt with.

I always forgive everyone for everything whenever I take communion, but I decided to do that on a certain day at a certain time.

Now the rest of the year I can keep short accounts. Now I only have to deal with recent events, anything that has happened before Easter Sunday 2012 is dealt with and doesn't have to be carried forward into the present.

My reading of the New Testament is going well. On the weekends I read something out of the Old Testament; whatever has life on it.

In Matthew 9:38 Jesus calls himself the Lord of the harvest.
In John 4:35 Jesus tells his disciples to look at the

fields and see that there are four months until harvest. Then he tells them to open their eyes and look at the people around them and see that they are ripe for harvest.

Jesus is able to open your eyes to see a harvest when you wouldn't normally be able to see it. The Bible is full of teaching about sowing and reaping and harvest time.

We have to be careful not to put a principle before a person, but we also have to realize that the Lord of the Harvest cannot have a harvest without seed being sown, without relying on the principle of sowing and reaping.

Mark 4:14
The farmer sows the word.

If you are reading the Bible you are a farmer of the word of God.

Luke 8:11
The seed is the word of God.

Luke 8:15
But the seed on good soil stands for those with a noble heart who hear the word and retain it and by persevering produce a crop.

You are also the good soil. You are God's field. And from you a harvest is produced; up to a hundredfold.

Thessalonians 2:13
And we also thank God continually because when you received the word of God, which you heard from us, you accepted it not as the word of men, but as it actually is, the word of God which is at work in you who believe.

You have to believe the word of God is at work in you. You have to decide you are expecting a harvest. You can't just go on reading the Bible year after year without getting a harvest.

Galatians 6:9
Let us not become weary in doing good, for at the proper time we will reap a harvest if we do not give up.

Are you weary? Have you given up?

Galatians 6:7
Do not be deceived, God cannot be mocked. A man reaps what he sows.

One way the enemy deceives us is by sowing bad seed into the same field we have sown good seed. Suddenly weeds appear and we are devastated.

This often happens in relationships. We may have sown good seed into a relationship for years. Next thing we notice is that some very bad seed is sprouting.

Don't be deceived, don't doubt, choose to ignore the weeds and focus on the good things that you can see. The other area where we can doubt is in the area of our health.

You might have prayed and believed and spoken the word of God and your health has gotten worse instead of better.

Once again two sorts of seed have been sown. The good seed which you have deposited into the situation, then the devil has come along and sown bad seed and these manifest in symptoms of sickness.

Then you stop believing because you think your prayers haven't worked or haven't been heard.

A few years ago Lorna broke her ankle. Since then she has had some pain and weakness in her ankle. For the last fourteen months, Lorna and I have been reading the bible and praying and speaking health into her ankle. And guess what?

A few weeks ago it suddenly got worse. It was stable for about six years and when we decide to sow the word of God into our hearts, her ankle gets worse not better.

So we are being tested. When you go to University you get tested.

Luke 8:13b
They believe for a while, but in the time of testing they fall away.

Now is our time of testing. We have to acknowledge the reality of the situation but we don't have to embrace the message behind it. It is a message of doubt and unbelief. Lorna and I have to believe we have crossed over into harvest time. You can't feed on the Bible and not produce a harvest of health.

Proverbs 4:20-22
My son pay attention to what I say; listen closely to my words, do not let them out of your sight, keep them within your heart; for they are life to those who find them and health to a man's whole body.

If you try and advance in the Kingdom of God you will find that the enemy also rises up to oppose you.

Mark 4:15

Some people are like seed along the path, where the word is sown. As soon as they hear it, Satan comes and takes away the word that was sown in them.

Did you know that as soon as you hear the word, Satan comes to steal it from your heart? We have to be alert and wake up to his schemes. In this house we are awake, we are alert, but it is still tempting to think it is all a coincidence, that the devil is not real, that he is not that active. For we are not unaware of his schemes.

One of the ways we can get the upper hand over the devil is to ask God for a fresh word of faith from heaven.

Lorna has just flown to Wellington, New Zealand to visit our son Samuel, who lives over there. The day before she had to fly out, she was at work and finding it very hard to stand up on her troublesome ankle.

When she came home and told me how bad it had become, you could see that she was very anxious. That night I opened my Bible and started to look for a word of encouragement. We got up the next morning for breakfast and I was able to tell her that I believed I had found a word for her.

I had found it in 1 Peter 2:25 *"But the word of the Lord stands forever."*

I told her about the word and said I believed it meant she would be able to stand up for as long as she needed to or wanted to. Today I have just received an e-mail from Lorna.

Hello Tony, I arrived safely, the flight was very good. My good news is that signs and wonders are accompanying your word for me; my foot is so much better, it's truly a miracle! I will stand forever. Thank you so much for your prayers. My pain level has gone right down, that is awesome. Tony isn't that wonderful? Take care, lots of love, Lorna.

Chapter 16

May 2012

I have just changed my mind about reading the Word of God. When I started this experiment I was reading the Bible out loud. Then I decided to read without speaking. Now I have changed back to reading the Bible out loud.

I just wasn't happy with the progress I was making. I couldn't feel the faith. I'm just impatient. I can't wait another 21 months for faith to manifest. I need it now. And the only way I know to get faith quickly is to read the scriptures out loud.

I have tried it all, praying, praising, worshipping, fasting, reading books, listening to tapes, going to conferences. These are all wonderful things to do and I should keep doing them.

But if I am desperate and need an answer from God where do I go and what do I do? I have already done it all. In the end I have concluded that even though God hears the cry of the heart, he always answers the prayer prayed in faith.

Jesus was never shy about commenting on people's faith level.

You have little faith.
I have not seen such great faith.
Your faith has healed you.
Why did you doubt?

As soon as I started again to read the word of God out loud I knew I was in a better place. With the same spirit of faith we also believe and therefore speak. I don't really understand why, I believe it works, I just believe.
Perhaps it works because I believe it does. I have not always been this convinced.

Now I am certain. In my mind the argument is won. The judge and jury have voted with me, "Do not let this Word depart from your mouth."

Chapter 17

June 2012

It is the end of the financial year and I am in my usual position at this time of year. It is also winter and my business does not like cold wet weather and neither do my customers. I have been doing the same business for about 25 years now. Every year when winter comes, my income goes down. Most of the year I am happy with my income, but there are always three or four months that disappoint. As you know I always tithe and give offerings.

I have always believed that Malachi 3:10-11 applies to a Christian when they tithe.

"So much blessing that you will not have room enough for it!"

My experience has always been the opposite. I have always had less work than I needed and therefore less money than I needed. I have listened to a thousand sermons on tithing and read many books on the subject of biblical finances.

My attitude has been to believe, even though I didn't see.

Recently I prayed to God, "Dear God, your promise in Malachi 3:10 has never been fulfilled in my finances, could you please show me the truth?"

A few days later my understanding opened up in a new way. This is the idea that I came up with. Right now I am tithing out of the Old Testament, why don't I try tithing out of the New Testament.

I am relying on Malachi 3:10-11.

Why don't I change that promise to another promise in 2 Corinthians 9:6-8.
"Remember this, whoever sows sparingly will also reap sparingly, and whoever sows generously will also reap generously."
Each man should give what his decided in his heart to give, not reluctantly or under compulsion.

For God loves a cheerful giver.

And God is able to make all grace abound to you so that in all things at all times having all that you need you will abound in every good work.

Malachi 3:10-11 promises blessing, but in Ephesians 1:3 it says that I have already been "blessed with every spiritual blessing."

Why do I need to rely on my tithing to give me blessing when I have already been blessed?

2 Corinthians 9:6-8 promises me grace.

Perhaps that's been my problem, I always thought I needed more blessing; maybe I have always needed more grace.

Blessing is like rain; it comes from above and waters your land. But grace is like a river or like an ocean; it causes your boat to float.

My friend is a sailor who has just renovated his yacht in his garage. He has painted it, put on a new mast and sails. He has poured out blessing on that yacht; it is blessed financially and physically.

But no matter how much blessing my friend John pours out onto that boat, the blessing will not make it float. He will have to put it on his trailer and take it to the harbour.

I will consider myself to be a rich man when I am debt free. I don't need a lot of money to live on to be happy. I just want to be financially free. Free from a mortgage and free from the banks.

How can you be free when you owe money? It's impossible.

You might say to me, "Don't stop giving offerings, the church needs your money."

My answer to that is, wouldn't it be better for the church in the long run if I paid my tithes and also paid off my debt? Then I will have even more money to give them.

Isn't it better for the minister if all his flock are debt free? Hasn't he got faith to live free of debt? C'mon pastor you can do it; you don't have to be dependent on debt either.

For with God nothing is impossible!

If grace works like the tide, then the tide can come in so high that it floats every boat. Some boats need more water under them than others.

Where sin abounds grace does much more abound.

Whatever level of debt someone has, it is possible for God's grace to flow into their lives to lift them up out of their situation into a better place.

The new has come the old has gone. What is old and obsolete is wasting away and it will soon disappear.

Chapter 18

July 2012

A good friend of mine has recently been dis-
inherited.

Is there such a word? I better say it more clearly;
he has lost his inheritance because his elderly
mother took offence when they had an argument!
My friend was never popular in his family.

He became a Christian and this put even more
distance between him and his mother and sister.

Romans 8:17
"Now if we are children, then we are heirs."

So my friend's mother is really saying to him, you
are no longer my son. Thank God that He will never
say to us that we are not His children.

Jesus told the parable of the prodigal son in Luke
15 to show us that even though we turn away from
God and waste our inheritance, if we repent and
return, he will forgive and restore us to our rightful
place.

Job 8:5-7
But if you will look to God and plead with the

Almighty, if you are pure and upright, even now he will rouse himself on your behalf and restore you to your rightful place.

Your beginnings will seem humble so prosperous will your future be.

I have mentioned before that as I am reading the New Testament it is becoming obvious that the central action is the cross but the central theme is the new agreement.

Luke 22:20
In the same way after the supper he took the cup, saying, this cup is the new agreement in my blood, which is poured out for you.

Our daily lives are built on many examples of a written agreement. Your driver's licence is a written agreement between you and the Government and police to allow you to drive a car on the road.

If you live on a farm you don't have to get anyone's permission to drive on the roads that are on your private property. If you are a son or daughter growing up on your parent's farm, you have to get their permission, but it is not written down, it is a verbal agreement.

The Bible is made up of many verbal agreements that God made with different people at different times and situations.

Adam and Eve had a verbal agreement with God not to eat the fruit from the tree of knowledge. They broke this agreement and paid the penalty.

Our driver's licence works the same; if we speed or drink drive we also pay the penalty. Even on your parents farm there are penalties even if they didn't write down the rules, those rules are still there. Some rules are unspoken because your parents think that you have inherited their common sense. When you are fifteen years old you haven't inherited anyone's common sense.

On our farm I was allowed to ride the motorbike and drive the new four wheel drive. My Father never ever said to me "Tony, don't knock over a tree with the 4WD!"

He never mentioned trees and driving in the same sentence.
There was a large old dead gumtree in one of our paddocks; it was rotten at the bottom. It was about 30 feet high. I drove up to it and gave it a nudge to knock it over.

Why not? It was dead. It would fall over easily.

I was right it did fall over easily.

I was trying to find reverse when it fell onto my father's new four wheel drive. It crushed the front of the vehicle and part of the roof. Suddenly I realized I had broken a rule that I never knew was there.

It was not written, it was not spoken but it sure existed.
When Moses came along God decided to write down every rule and law that existed.

Moses wrote down spoken rules and unspoken rules so everyone would be quite clear about what was expected of them. We call them the law and the commandments.

The old agreement under Moses works like this.
"If you behave you will receive."

The new agreement under Jesus changed all that, it says
"If you believe you will receive."

The old agreement under Moses depended on how hard you worked.

Paul sums it up in Galatians 3:10, *all who rely on observing the law are under a curse, for it is written; "Cursed is everyone who does not continue to do everything written in the book of the Law."*

The new agreement under Jesus depends on believing.

John 6: 28-29
"What must we do to do the works God requires?" Jesus answered, "The work of God is this; to believe in the one he has sent!"

I have mentioned earlier that the floods that happened to Brisbane tore people's lives apart. Most people had an insurance policy; the problem was that a lot of the insurance policies did not cover people for flooding.

Or if they did cover them for flooding, it was storm water flooding or river flooding; not both.

Some people were flooded because water backed up in the storm water pipes and others just by the river rising. What was confusing for the people was the insurance companies used different measurements to decide what was storm water and what was the river causing the flood. There were a number of people who just weren't covered for flooding at all.

Now the insurance companies have brought out new policies. These new policies (new agreements) cover all flooding however it happens. Everyone gets the same policy so that there is certainty.

I received a notice from my insurance company telling me that I am covered for flooding. I live on a hill, miles from any river or storm water problem. It's impossible for my house to flood. There was such bad publicity for these companies because of the Brisbane floods that they have now gone to the extreme.

Under the Law of Moses people were never sure whether they had been good enough. People never knew whether they worked hard enough for long enough. There was a problem with doubt and uncertainty.

Hebrews 8:7
For if there had been nothing wrong with the first covenant (agreement), no place would have been sought for another.

If the insurance agreements had worked perfectly when Brisbane was flooded the companies would not have introduced new policies.

But they didn't work; a lot of people's lives were ruined.

So now we all have new insurance policies, these new policies are better than the old ones because they are based on better promises.

They promise that if your house is destroyed by any flood of any type, your house will be repaired, renewed and restored. Guess what? You will be revived; you won't be depressed and stressed as you were before.

Job 36:16
He is wooing you from the jaws of distress to a spacious place free from restriction.

The new agreement that Jesus has given us is superior to the old agreement Moses gave us, because it is based on better promises.

Moses - Only behave.
Jesus - Only believe.

John 1: 17
For the law came through Moses, grace and truth came through Jesus.

Here's the downside of the new insurance policy, they are a lot more expensive. It makes sense doesn't it? The more you pay the better the result.

Now here is an unwritten law that we all believe.
"You pay for quality!"
"Nothing comes cheap!"

When Moses proclaimed every commandment of the law he used the blood of animals. When Jesus speaks to his disciples at the last supper he says; "This cup is the new agreement in my blood."

You have an insurance policy with God himself. His son, the Lord Jesus Christ came to earth to organise it and bring it to pass through his death on the cross.

He shed His blood to pay the price for this new agreement.

Isaiah NKJ 59:19b
When the enemy comes in like a flood, the spirit of the Lord will lift up a standard against him.

If there are floods in Brisbane again, the people will be able to face those floods in faith instead of fear because everyone knows that their insurance policy covers them for flood.

We have the same assurance and certainty because we also have a legal document, recognised by the courts of heaven. A legal policy organised by Jesus himself. A policy document paid for by Jesus in his own blood.

A few years ago the glass in our shower cracked. It is a special laminated glass and is expensive to replace.
I had not read my house insurance policy before, because we had never used it to claim anything. As I started to read the document I saw these words, "Glass shower doors are covered in this policy." Instantly my attitude changed. My shower door was replaced for free.

If earthly policy documents work like that, how much more should policy documents that are organised from heaven work? If you were reading your earthly insurance policy and came across these words.
"Your insurance company will supply all your needs."

You would think what a great company, what a great attitude. How much happier should we be when we open the Bible and read these words.

Philippians 4:19
And my God will meet all your needs according to His glorious riches in Christ Jesus.

Chapter 19

August 2012

Lorna and I have just come home after going to my church and hearing a great sermon. The subject of the sermon was repentance. The Pastor told us that repentance is the foundation of our faith.

He quoted Hebrews 6:1: *therefore let us leave the elementary truths about Christ and go on to maturity, not laying again the foundation of repentance from acts that lead to death (or from useless rituals).*

My wife says I need to repent from my pride and become willing to accept any invitations or opportunities that come my way; she means that I have to be willing to say yes instead of no.

She is quoting Isaiah 1:19, *"If you are willing and obedient, you will eat the best from the land!"*

My reply is Romans 6:14, *"I am not under the law, but under grace."*

In the gospel of Mark 14:1-9 there is a story of a woman who broke a jar of perfume and poured it on the head of Jesus.

Now some of the people who were watching this happen judged her and said she was wasting the perfume because it could have been sold and the money given to the poor.

The law will always tell you what you are not doing, but grace will always tell you that what you are doing is good enough.

Jesus told these people to leave her alone. "You will always have the poor but you will not always have me!"

She was preparing Jesus for His burial.

One group of people thought she was short-sighted while Jesus thought she was long-sighted.
He said, "She did what she could!"

A friend of mine who is a lawyer was asked to speak at church and share with the people. The story he told was very encouraging.

A few weeks later I was having a coffee with him and he happened to mention that there were probably some people in church that morning thinking, why is he up there speaking?

I said to my friend "Where did that thought come from? It is a thought from the enemy."

I told my friend, "We are never good enough and we have never done enough, but Jesus is good enough and He has done enough."

The devil will always argue with these negative thoughts.

We can admit that we aren't good enough and we haven't done enough but we can turn the argument around and say that Jesus is good enough and he has done more than enough by dying for us on the cross.

We can then declare that when we believed in Jesus and accepted him into our heart; we also had done enough.

There is only one test that you have to pass in life and that test is found in 2 Corinthians 13:5.
"Examine yourselves to see whether you are in the faith; test yourselves."
Do you not realize that Christ Jesus is in you – unless of course you fail the test?

If you have believed in Jesus, then Christ lives in you by His Spirit. You have passed the test, you have not failed.

Grace is an attitude that always helps you look good.
Law is an attitude that always makes you look bad.

Lorna took some soup to a lady who had a new baby at home. The young lady's mother was also there. Lorna had not put any cream or milk into the pumpkin soup. The young mother ate the soup for lunch and thoroughly enjoyed it.

The young mother and her mother praised Lorna for being so thoughtful by not adding cream or milk to the soup, because the young mother was experimenting to see if eliminating dairy in her diet would possibly help the baby settle at night.

Lorna had no idea the young mother had decided to go on a dairy free diet.

Grace causes you to accidently get things the right way round. Under the law everything you do is wrong. Grace tells me that just turning up for church is enough.
Grace tells me that it doesn't matter how much money I give as long as I give cheerfully. Grace tells me that as long as I say yes to some opportunities that is enough.

Law says you are not doing enough in the church. Law says you are not giving enough money. Law says you are not saying yes often enough.

I like Romans 6:14 because it tells me that I am not under law, but under grace.

This world worships success and I have to admit I have worshipped at the altar of success. But if you have believed in Jesus you have passed the only test that matters.

You have not failed, you have succeeded.

When I went to high school, year 12 was very tough because it had a very hard test at the end of the year.

You passed or you failed. There was no in between. We did the exam in November and you did not get the results until January.

When the results came out all my classmates and friends were waiting down at the local hotel. When I walked in the front door there was a table to the left with all the people who had failed and there was a table to the right with all the people who had passed.

As I opened the door all the people on the table to the left yelled out to me, "Tony come over here!" They always believed I would fail and they were right.

I also believed I would fail because I had not worked hard enough. What they didn't know was that morning when the envelope arrived in the mail and I opened it, there was a big surprise.
It said "PASS".
I said to my friends, "I can't join you because I passed, I didn't fail!"

I turned to the right and joined the table of winners.

This is the story behind the story. My physics teacher that year was on the state board of examiners. He helped set the exam questions.

When I sat down to do my three hour physics exam many of the questions looked familiar. We had done these same questions many times that year and this enabled me to get a high score in physics which caused me to pass the whole exam in year 12.

I could now go to university if I wanted.

This is how God's grace works behind the scene to lead you to Jesus. He gives you the ability to repent and believe and all you have to do is say yes.

Because you say yes; you have passed the biggest exam of the universe, you are now going to heaven. You have passed from hell to heaven. You have succeeded in the most important test you will ever face.

My son and daughter would both say in jest that they were the smartest. It was a family joke. Our family had a funny way to express this.

We would say "Who is the sharpest tool in the shed?"

When they did their last year in high school they both received exactly the same results. So the humorous talk at the family dinner table was that they were both equally as smart as each other, this appeared to put the bantering to rest.

Sam and Jess have always thought they were smarter than their mother and father. How can you convince your children that you are smarter than them?

My wife Lorna is the most loving person I have ever met, the family have always known this and our friends at the local church have always remarked about how loving Lorna is. She has an enormous mercy gift. She is always visiting people and encouraging them, she sends them gifts and she really does care.

One night at the family dinner table, the four of us were once again joking about who was the sharpest tool in the shed?

All of a sudden I realized that Lorna was the smartest person in the family because she was the most loving person in the family. She is the most loving person any of us have ever known.

We had always acknowledged this but what we hadn't realized was that the smartest thing you can ever do in your life is love someone.

1 Corinthians 1:19b-20 *"the intelligence of the intelligent I will frustrate."*
Where is the wise man?
Where is the scholar?
Where is the philosopher of this age?

The Bible talks to the smartest people on earth and tells them if they are not loving, they are not smart.

1 Corinthians 13:13
But the greatest of these is love.

When the woman came into the room to pour perfume on Jesus, the people in the room didn't show her any love, they operated with an attitude of law.

But Jesus loved her and showed her an attitude of grace. The law will design a test and make sure you fail.
Grace will design a test to make sure you succeed. The argument that you have never done enough and you will never be good enough is a destructive thought pattern that needs to be torn down.

2 Corinthians 10:4
The weapons we fight with are not weapons of the world.

On the contrary they have divine power to demolish arguments and every thought that sets itself up against the knowledge of God, and we take captive every thought to make it obedient to Christ.

We need to argue that Jesus is good enough and he has done enough.
Then we need to declare that when we believed in Jesus we did all that we ever needed to do. The smartest thing a human being can do on this planet is to believe in Jesus and receive him into their

heart. You are now the smartest person, because to believe in someone is to love them.

Chapter 20

September 2012

When I was a young preacher in Adelaide I received an invitation to speak at the Sunday morning service of a church that was situated near the Red Light district in Adelaide.

It was pastored by a couple who in their past lives had been a prostitute and a bank robber. They were now both saved and in ministry.

I spoke about the story of David and Bathsheba in 2 Samuel chapters 11 and 12, they had committed adultery that resulted in the birth of a son, the son got sick and died. When I preached that morning I spoke about the unusual behaviour of David.

2 Samuel 12:21-23
His servants asked him, "Why are you acting this way? While the child was alive you fasted and wept, but now that the child is dead you get up and eat!"

He answered," While the child was alive I fasted and wept. I thought," Who knows? The Lord may be gracious to me and let the child live.

But now that he is dead why should I fast? Can I bring him back again? I will go to him but he will not return to me."

I didn't know there was a married couple in the service who had lost a young child. When I finished speaking they came up to me and told me their story. They had been encouraged because they felt God had moved me to mention that story to let them know God was aware of their pain and suffering. They really believed that God cared about them.

My wife met a lady who had lost her son in his early twenties. This lady told Lorna that she had received a supernatural peace that passed all understanding.
It was so powerful that she didn't experience any pain or grief, it was incredible. To this day her heart and mind have been kept in that beautiful state of peace and rest. That's one of the most powerful statements I have ever heard.

God does care about the saved and the unsaved people. A few weeks ago I was at a customer's house, a couple in their early sixties.

They had been through a real trial. The husband had just survived bowel cancer and now he had found out that he had prostate cancer. The wife had received a heart transplant. She had just spent sixty days in hospital.

They had been my customers for fifteen years and I had witnessed to them in the past. After I finished my work I sat down with them and was able to explain the difference between earning your salvation and receiving your salvation by grace.

Sometimes when you talk to people about God you feel your words go right into them. This was one of those days. It's amazing how patient God is, at the same time their need to accept Jesus into their hearts couldn't be more urgent!

CONGRATULATIONS TO ME!

I have just passed the half way mark. I have been doing my experiment for over 18 months. If God is invited into our projects He can take something that is half-finished and cause it to start working before its time.

The disciples had a similar experience with Jesus.
John 6:19
When they had rowed three or three and a half miles, they saw Jesus approaching the boat walking on the water, and they were terrified.

John 6:21
Then they were willing to take Him into the boat,
and immediately the boat reached the shore where
they were heading.

Notice that they were willing to invite Jesus into
what they were doing and suddenly they were at
their destination.

A few weeks ago I flew over to Wellington, New
Zealand to visit my son Samuel. I had this funny
thought that I should download my writings onto a
memory stick or (usb flash drive) in case I sat next
to someone on the plane and had one of those God
conversations, I could just hand them the usb stick.
They could then read my story later on.

On the flight over to Wellington there was only one
spare seat on the whole plane, it was right next to
me. I didn't have a conversation with anyone!

Sometimes one thought leads to another. I said to
Samuel, "What do you think about putting my half-
finished writings on the internet so anyone I meet
could look it up and read it?"

Samuel told me it was probably a good idea
because it would force me to lift my standards

since people outside the family would be reading my story for the first time.

Samuel had a similar experience. He had been playing his guitar at an Italian Restaurant in Wellington. This had caused him to lift his standard of playing and presentation.

Exposing yourself to a wider audience and your peers is a good idea if you can cope with people's responses. Fortunately for me the response has been very encouraging.

When I got home I organised a website, something that I had no experience in doing and then told a few of the men I knew.

Here is the response I received from an old friend of mine who lives in Adelaide. He has a lot of experience as a minister; he is also an author of two books.

Hi Tony, Hi Lorna,
I read your story this morning, and really enjoyed it. It's a great idea to diarise your progress over three years. Your humour comes through, very droll. Your honesty is refreshing and brave. The lessons you have learnt over the years are really valuable; I gained much from all your insights in the word, and

*from your spiritual evolutions particularly I enjoyed
all your poignant little stories.
Well done my friend, Paul Godrich.*

This was my first response from anyone, I am glad
it came in first. Thanks to everyone for their
encouragement.

In the meantime I was able to talk Lorna into doing
her own website. Four weeks ago Lorna and I
would have never believed or known that we
would put our writings out in the public domain.

I was thinking I might put it into a small book for
the family. I thought if anything was going to
happen it would happen after the three years had
passed. This is a quote from a book I have been
reading.

*"No-one around us seemed to have faith for
anything out of the ordinary."*

The angel told Daniel that God was involved from
the first day of his project.

The angel told Daniel, *"Do not be afraid Daniel.
Since the first day you set your mind to gain
understanding and to humble yourself before your
God, your words were heard, and I have come in*

response to them."
Daniel 10:11

We never know when God will turn up. The disciples were willing to take Jesus into the boat, and then they were immediately at their destination.

I once saw a funny video showing a man playing baseball; he hits a home run but doesn't know it and starts to run to first base, then to second base. Men on the other team start chasing him; he thinks they are chasing him to get him out. But they are chasing him to tell him to stop running; they were trying to tell him the good news.

I have been doing my Bible reading with my eyes on a three year goal. Meanwhile I have an idea to do something in the present. For many people it is not a new idea to put your writings on a website, but for me it was a brand new idea and it was for now and not for later.

An experience I had in Bible College illustrates this dilemma. The Bible College I attended had, in years past, seen a move of God more than once. The year I was in college was in 1981, we had a visit from a pastor who came from Nagaland.

It is a state in the north-eastern part of India with a population of just under two million people. Revivals have taken place in 1956, 1966, and 1972. The result is that Nagaland is a predominately Christian state.

This pastor taught in our college for a few days. Not long after, we experienced a move of the Holy Spirit; this began at morning chapel and went for a few hours.

After this happened the pastor in charge of the college called us all together and asked the students if we would like to take a break from lectures and normal duties to seek God.

We had a vote, the majority voted against the idea. Can you believe this? We are in college to learn about God but when we get the opportunity to experience God the majority vote against it?

The reason they did this was because they had their eyes on finishing their studies. They missed the opportunity when it came.

In Luke 19: 41-44 Jesus wept as he made his entrance into the city of Jerusalem because they did not recognise the time of God's coming.

You diligently study the scriptures because you think that by them you possess eternal life. These are the scriptures that testify about me, yet you refuse to come to me to have life.
John 5:39

Acts 8:26-40 tells the story of a man in his chariot who is reading the Bible out loud. Suddenly Phillip the evangelist approaches him and explains to him who the words are referring to. This man gives the order to stop the chariot and says, "Look here is water why shouldn't I be baptised?"
He broke his gaze from future events and stepped into God's plan for the present.

When the opportunity comes don't let it slide!

Chapter 21

October 2012

There is a change happening. Up until now the emphasis has been on reading and speaking the word of God. Now I have felt a subtle shift towards spending time in God's presence.

Recently I lifted my hands in worship at church. I normally don't do that. But I felt an unlocking in my heart. My wife is a presence person and I am a word person.

It can appear that women can sense God's presence easier than men because they are intuitive.

Speaking in tongues has come back in a big way. Now when I read the Bible, I quietly and slowly pray in tongues. It is two for the price of one. I am reading and praying at the same time.

Jackie Pullinger's book *Chasing the Dragon* tells how Jackie would pray in tongues before going out onto the street to witness and pray for people in Hong Kong.

She said, "Using the gift of tongues opened a new door. Because I was praying in the Holy Spirit, God was able to lead me, to people he had prepared."

I have been praying in tongues a lot over the past month. Two weeks ago I got the urge to go into the city centre on Sunday morning to pray and witness to people.

I also got the idea to do a new website called prayerforfree.com. When I pray for people or meet them for the first time, I tell them to put a prayer request on the website so I can pray for them and it gives us an opportunity to continue to connect.

The people I pray for can let me know how they are going and if God is answering their prayers.

I have gone into Brisbane city for the last three Sundays. I go in at 8am and walk around talking to people for 1-2 hours.

I have filled myself up with the word and prayer; it was about time I gave something back out into the community.

Some of the people I have met are young men who are from overseas. They are a long way from home. It is a good idea to pray for their needs and circumstances.

Hopefully God will bless what I am doing.

There are a lot of people who haven't heard the gospel. I would enjoy sharing the good news of salvation with them.

In 1979 my parents asked me to leave home, later on they asked me to leave the state.

I left Adelaide and went to Melbourne to share a unit with a school friend called Jack. I was able to get a job with a fabric supplier in the city centre of Melbourne.

At my new job there was a salesman called Monty who invited me to have dinner with his wife Heather and their young sons. Heather and Monty told me they were born again Christians. I had heard that expression only once before that night.

They told me I could be saved right there in their house. I said, "No thanks."

On the train as I went home that night, I was alone in the carriage. A deep brooding and foreboding came over me; I felt God was trying to speak to me. It was scary. The impression I received was that if I rejected Him and went my own way I would suffer the consequences.

I knew what the result of going my own way would be. Myself and everyone around me had suffered because of my behaviour and the future looked bleak and since being in Melbourne the bad cycle had started all over again but it was worse than before.

When I got off the train and walked home I looked up at the moon and said, "Okay God I'm yours." That's all I said. I went to work for the rest of the week basically forgetting about what had happened and what I had said.

On Saturday night, Jack went out to a party while I stayed home. Later that night, I was sitting on a bean bag on the floor of our lounge room listening to a tape Monty had given me.

Suddenly I sensed someone come into the room and stand at my side. I couldn't believe what was happening to me. No-one had told me about these things.

A person and a presence came into that room. I immediately knew it was Jesus. I could feel this incredible love flow from Him to me. I was in tears and happy at the same time. My mind was stable and sober. However, around me in that room there was a brightness and a peace.

I stayed in that atmosphere for about three hours, and then Jack came home from the party. I told Jack what had happened to me, he was a bit under the influence and couldn't understand what I was saying.

The next morning I had arranged to go to Heather and Monty's house and then visit their church. When I arrived at their house, I told them my story, they just stood there smiling.

"Do you think I've been born again?" I said. They definitely believed I had been born again. I had become a Christian. They happily took me to church that Sunday.

I enjoyed the service so next week I was baptised in water and baptised in the Holy Spirit. While I was still in the baptismal water the Pastor prayed for me to be baptised in the Holy Spirit. I didn't know what that was; it was another term I had never heard before.
Next minute I was shouting out some strange language and everyone around me starts rejoicing.

They all thought this was wonderful. I felt wonderful and stayed on a high which lasted for months. It really was true what they said about Jesus. He is the truth. He is real.

What would have happened to me if Monty and Heather had not invited me over for dinner and witnessed to me? Would someone else have done it if they had not?

My old friends didn't like me getting saved and we all drifted apart. One of those friends was called Russell. I didn't hear from him for about 14 years. I rang him after all that time had passed. He was doing well. I asked him if Christians had witnessed to him in those 14 years. He said they had not.

It seemed I was the only person on the planet who had told him about getting saved and becoming a Christian. No-one in all that time had approached him about his eternal destiny.

I have always believed that if I didn't witness to a person then someone else would.
Who wants to wear that responsibility?

I am glad to have the opportunity to go into the city centre on Sunday mornings to speak to people about God.

News flash!

We have just arrived home from the city centre. Lorna went over to a man who was limping and in pain. She prayed and the pain went immediately.

What a great result. The man was very surprised and very grateful.

Sunday morning.

My wife Lorna and I are sitting on a seat in the shopping mall. We have just prayed and asked God who we should pray for before we go home. A minute later a window cleaner walks past us carrying his equipment. He is limping and looks like he is in pain. Lorna goes over to him and asks if she can pray for his leg. As soon as she starts to pray he says, "The pain is gone, the pain is gone!"

Sunday morning a few weeks later.

We are again in the city centre and we meet up with the window cleaner, his name is Neil. We asked him how he was going.

This is his reply, "I have a fused hip and have been in pain for 14 years. I have been taking pain tablets for 14 years. Since you prayed for me I have had no pain and no pain tablets. Because I have no pain my business has grown as I can do more work."

How did Lorna and I end up praying for the sick and seeing them healed?

Chapter 22

November 2012

Today, you can change everything by activating your faith. The Bible will work if you mix it with faith. Things work if you believe. I am proving right now that the Bible has the power to turn a person into a success.

God will do it. Just believe that reading the Bible changes you and your situation. If you believe it works; then it works.

This is a story that is happening right now.

I am using my own life as an example. Simply believe that reading the Bible will create faith. The decision is yours.

Cross over today into a new realm of faith. Turn your believing switch on now! Say yes to God's complete and full plan for your life.

What you are about to read can change your believing.

James 1:6-8
But when he asks, he must believe and not

doubt, because he who doubts is like a wave of the sea, blown and tossed by the wind. That man should not think he will receive anything from the Lord; he is a double-minded man, unstable in all he does.

This is how to unlock your faith. You must eliminate all doubt! And we eliminate doubt by choosing long term results over short term results.

Abraham doubted that he would have a son by Sarah; so he slept with Hagar. The short term result was not a happy one.

But God had something better in mind. Abraham had to choose to believe in God's plan even though it would take 25 years.

We have to involve ourselves in spiritual activities that last. Then we don't doubt. Doubt wants it now; faith has a long term view.

We have to find something that we can believe in 100 per cent. As Christians we have already found someone we can believe in. Now all we have to do is find some spiritual activity that works.
We don't doubt that it works, even when it appears not to work.

For everyone this activity will take a different form.

Abraham and Sarah had to learn how to believe for a child and not doubt. This took them years to achieve.

The activity I have chosen; is to read the Word of God and speak it as I read.

Faith comes by hearing the Word.

A long time ago God told me, "Do not let this Word depart from your mouth."
You would have noticed that I have been quite double-minded about this matter up till now.

Not anymore. I am going to do this without wavering.

Week after week, not being diverted, not allowing a new idea to cause me to doubt. I will prove that this works. You must believe that it works; for it to succeed.
Yes, this is the secret of faith – to believe in something 100 per cent without any doubt. No wavering. This is what I have discovered over the last 18 months.

I have finally come to the place where this is settled in my head and in my heart. Different people will choose a different activity, but the attitude has to be all believing and no doubt!

What has God asked you to do? Settle it in your mind and heart. Choose the long term over the short term. Do not be double-minded. Produce an Isaac. He who laughs last laughs loudest.

Abraham and Sarah are still laughing every time someone becomes a Christian because they also become a son or daughter of Abraham. That is an excellent long term result. Abraham is still being rewarded for his victory over doubt.

Jesus said, "Stop doubting and believe!"

I have finally heard him.

Chapter 23

December 2012

You are joining me for the second half of my three year journey. Today is the first Sunday in December 2012.
Hello to everyone; I hope that God is building up your faith.

I recently read an article about Richard Branson and his struggle to start his new airline. He was opposed by the other more established airlines. They organised an attack against him and his airline. His enemies had organised a dirty tricks unit that was illegal. He had to stand up to his opposition.

The decision to let Virgin Atlantic operate at Heathrow in competition with British Airways became the trigger for BA's so-called dirty tricks campaign against Virgin. Branson sued British Airways for libel.

BA settled out of court when its lawyers discovered the lengths to which the company had gone in trying to kill off Virgin.

The most dangerous times for a business project is in the first couple of years.

In the book of Ezra the Jews had returned to Jerusalem and were trying to rebuild the temple, but their enemies were opposing them.

Ezra 4:4
Then the people around them set out to discourage the people of Judah and make them afraid to go on building.
They hired counsellors to work against them and frustrate their plans.

Because we have been reading the Bible, our spirits have become quite strong. We are normally very peaceful and easy going people. Recently we have changed. We have been spending a lot of time resisting the devil in prayer. I think our authority has increased.

We submit ourselves to God and then we resist the devil. We expect the devil's influence to decrease and we expect God's influence to increase in our lives and over our family.

We have seen some evidence of this. Some of our families work situations have changed for the better.

Lorna and I have experienced a lot of opposition from people and circumstances over the years. It seems that we have been in a constant battle. We don't find it easy to take authority in prayer. There comes a time in your life when you can't ignore the schemes of your opponents any longer and you have to rise up and address the problem.

Ephesians 6:1
We are not fighting against humans. We are fighting against forces and authorities and against rulers of darkness and powers in the spiritual world.

This decision to fight or not to fight can be confusing.

What we have noticed lately is the desire to stand up for our legal rights in prayer is coming from our spirit within us rather than our mind.

Here is some good news. I have been praying for you the reader. I use Psalm 23 as a pattern for prayer. So once you have read my story you are getting prayed for. I pray for all the readers. Will I do this forever? I don't know, it is just one of those things that I find myself doing. It has become a natural thing for me.

Here is an example of the way I use Psalm 23 as a pattern of prayer.

Dear Father,
I pray that you will bless every person that is
reading my story. I ask that you Lord Jesus would
be their shepherd. That you would shepherd them out of doubt and
into a new level of faith. Please supply all their
needs.
Give them grace, strength and wisdom. Cause the
people reading my story to lie down in green
pastures of success. Deliver them from every
spiritual and emotional storm. Restore their
relationships, health and finances.

Guide them in a path of right decisions under the
authority of the name of Jesus. Let the law of the
spirit of life set them free. May (resurrection) life
be their experience. I command every evil spirit
that has been harassing and opposing them to be
removed.
Strengthen them in their spirit, so they will feel
your strong support.

Enable them to sit down at the table you have
prepared. Let it be a meal of the word of God. I ask
Father that you anoint the reader so they would
know the truth and the truth would set them free!
Fill them up with faith so that something good will

happen to them. And bless them in their church life.

Are you glad that you read this chapter?

Remember Psalm 23. Believe for this to come to pass in your life. Why don't you join me in praying the words of this Psalm out over your life and the lives of your friends and family? It sounds like a plan!

Jeremiah 29:11
For I know the plans I have for you declares the Lord. Plans to prosper you and not to harm you. Plans to give you a hope and a future.

Chapter 24

January 2013

It is Tuesday, the first day of 2013. I am nearly into my third year. I have found the word of God is building up Lorna and myself. We are in a much better place than we were two years ago. This year I am going to add more prayer into my routine.

When we pray we are inviting the Holy Spirit into our lives to open our eyes. I often use a lighthouse as an example. It is built on rock as the foundation. As it is built; it rises higher and higher. The reason for all this effort is to put a very bright light on the top of the lighthouse.

The purpose of this light is to help the ships avoid danger and find their way through a storm in safety.
When we are baptised in the Holy Spirit and given the gift of prayer in tongues we are given the ability to shine brightly like a lamp so that we can see our way out of danger and trouble into a better place.

So this year I am going to include praying in the Holy Spirit [praying in tongues] in my routine so I can become aware of the benefits of this gift. Last year around September and October I spent a lot of time praying in tongues as I read my Bible.

I noticed that after a short period of time Lorna and I felt moved to go into the city centre to pray and witness to people. We saw some very good results. I also noticed around that time that the response to my website increased and people sent in some very encouraging messages about how God had blessed them as they read my story.

That is one of the things I like about praying in tongues; you are allowing the Holy Spirit to pray through you for anyone, anywhere in the world. You may not know the person or their circumstances or the answer to their problem but the Holy Spirit does.

He knows how to guide us out of danger into a place of peace and protection. He knows how to change us into people of wisdom and authority. He knows how to deliver us out of failure into success. And He knows how to make a barren person into a fruitful person.

Many years ago we spent a lot of time praying in the Holy Spirit; by the end of that year nearly every circumstance in our lives had changed for the better.

We crossed over into a wonderful time of harvest. Great doors of opportunity opened for us. We had one of our best holidays ever.

Our finances were greatly blessed; we just entered into a time of real happiness. When the lights go on you can easily find your way into a place of blessing. When it is dark we don't know where to go or what to do. I am hoping for this year to be a year when the lights go on.

Genesis 37 tells the story of Joseph. As a young man who is falsely accused by Potiphar's wife, Joseph ends up in prison. Two of his fellow inmates have dreams and no understanding of what their dreams mean. Joseph has the ability to interpret dreams. He tells the men the meaning of their dreams.

What Joseph says comes to pass. When Pharaoh has two dreams that he cannot understand, he calls Joseph out of prison to interpret his dreams. Joseph interprets the dreams and is promoted by Pharaoh and put in charge of Egypt. All these men were in the dark, they could not understand their dreams.

Joseph came along and shone a very bright light into their situation. Joseph gave them understanding.

When understanding comes it is the same as bringing a bright light into a dark place. Joseph was promoted because of his ability to shine the light of understanding into a dark situation and make everything clear. At the start no-one knows what to do and how to do it.

The next moment Joseph has shown them what is going to happen and how to deal with the problem. He had a plan from heaven.

Many years later Joseph told his brothers.

Genesis 50:19
"Don't be afraid. You intended to harm me but God intended it for good! To accomplish what is now being done, the saving of many lives."

I pray that God will open our minds so that we can understand the scripture below and recognise our harvest when it arrives.

John 4:35
Open your eyes and look at the fields! They are ripe for harvest.

Chapter 25

February 2013

I have now officially completed two years of my journey through the New Testament. I have become very aware that the Bible is food for my spirit. My body needs three meals a day to stay strong because I do physical work. My mind loves to read a good book or watch a great movie.

I also enjoy reading the newspaper. Information is food for my mind. It is my spirit that is getting the most benefit from reading the Bible.

Thessalonians 5:23
May your whole spirit, soul and body be kept blameless.

Paul talks about the need for our spirit, soul and body to be kept blameless. But I want to talk about the benefits of our spirit being well fed. We feed our mind and our body in a very regular way. When we feed our mind it grows strong, when we feed our body it gains energy.
When we feed our spirit it also grows strong and gains energy.

I read a book recently about a man who had never seen a healing. He decided to fast 10 days a month and he did this for five months. One day he sensed he should pray for a lady's healing. Something in him rose up! I believe that was his spirit rising up to do what he couldn't do before.

Fasting weakens the soul and body, it then enables your spirit to dominate and do what you could not normally do if your mind or body had their way. Jesus told the disciples to pray because the spirit is willing but the body is weak. The disciples were exhausted; they fell into a deep sleep.

But Jesus knew that there was a huge challenge in front of them. They needed to be ready and alert. They needed to keep their lamps burning. When we light a lamp we don't put it under a bowl. When our spirit lights up, we shouldn't put it under the influence of our soul.

Our spirit with the help of the Holy Spirit is in charge of our lives. We should always be spirit led people. And the Holy Spirit leads us by our spirit not by our mind. Some people have fed their minds all their lives, but have not fed their spirit. Their spirit needs spiritual food. The Bible is food for our spirit.

I can sense my spirit getting stronger. I am learning to make decisions based on what my spirit senses is right rather than on what my mind thinks.

I have seen television documentaries of people who are trying to raise old boats or aircraft or other heavyweight objects off the ocean floor so they can recover them.

The way they do this is to get an underwater balloon and attach it to the heavy object that is stuck on the ocean floor. The power that is needed is huge because the ocean floor won't let go easily; and also the object they want to lift weighs many tons.

After they get everything in place, they then begin to inflate the balloon with bubbles of air. Slowly the air fills up the balloon. The air filled balloon is now more powerful than the ocean floor. The balloon wins as the ocean floor lets go and this very heavy piece of equipment starts to rise to the surface.

This is what is happening to your spirit when you read the Bible. Imagine every word from the Bible is full of the breath of God. Slowly your spirit is being filled with the life of God. This world tries to hold us down by appealing to our soul's desires or fears.

The lust of the eyes and the pride of what we own and possess. Our physical body demands our attention all day long. Our soul and our body belong to this world; but our spirit belongs on a higher level in Gods kingdom.

As we fill our spirit with the life of God, we find our spirit rising up to a new level. We can experience a new increase of energy. Now our spirit is powerful enough to drag our soul and body up to a better level of behaviour. We are no longer stuck in the soul's mud of normal existence.

Our spirit always reaches out to God. Now we are free from what has bound us in the past. The law of the spirit of life has set us free. Jesus said, "The spirit is willing but the body is weak."

Proverbs says, "*A man's spirit sustains him.*"
Holds him up!

Here is a story about a woman who felt in her spirit to obey God but was held back by her mind (soul). She was worried about what people would think!

Edward Millar was involved in the Argentinean revival. In 1973 he was speaking at a conference, he told how the revival began. He was a missionary from America to Argentina.

The mission's board stopped his support when they heard he was no longer distributing tracts but rather spending whole days in prayer.

He felt he should convene a prayer meeting. Only a handful of people arrived. Even then he was the only one prepared to pray.

One young woman came every night. However, she prayed not one word. Ed attempted to find out why God asked him to call the meeting.

He asked if anyone felt to do anything. The young woman replied she felt like striking the table. She wouldn't do it, however. She said she felt foolish doing something that carried such little significance.

After three nights (and nothing happening) she was finally persuaded to hit the table. Millar suggested they all walk around the table and strike it, one after another.

When the particular woman finally hit it, the room filled with the glory of God.

They all spent hours in the presence of the Lord. From that point, a great revival broke out in Argentina with literally hundreds of thousands turning to Christ.

During the revival, an enormous number of miracles happened through evangelist Tommy Hicks.

Although a woman hitting a table obviously is not the only element triggering a revival of these proportions, Edward Millar felt her obedience played a part in releasing a move of the Holy Spirit.

Chapter 26

March 2013

My friend has changed his job. He has gone from a company that earned its money from government contracts, to another company that earns its money in a similar way. But there is a difference. The company he has just left earned its money after it performed its duties.

His new job is with a company that is paid by the government before it does the work. One is paid before it does the work the other is paid after it does the work.
Can you imagine that the atmosphere is different?

It is much more relaxed, everyone is happier, the pressure is not as intense. The motivation is different. The staff are motivated because they are happy. At the old job the staff were motivated by threats.

Today is our 30th wedding anniversary. We are both very happy. Some people are not happy in their marriage. Things have not gone well for them.

One advantage Lorna and I have is the way our relationship was built; it has enabled us not to doubt.

We have always believed that God organised our relationship.

The thought or idea that God was involved means that we can believe we were meant to be together. When you believe you are meant to be together you can stand against doubt.

And we all know that doubts do come. Some people doubt that they are meant to be together and this causes problems to grow. If you or someone you know has suffered a relationship breakdown, it is very important to get them motivated again and keep them motivated.

Here is a good place to start.

Luke 1:45
Blessed is she (he) who has believed that what the Lord has said to her (him) will be accomplished!

Every relationship is built on people keeping their word. When they don't keep their word or promises something breaks. So we have to repair what is broken and we do that by peeling away all the lies, doubts, and broken promises until we have to look away from people and look at what God has said.

If God has said it, then it will happen, but we have to believe that what He says will happen. God's part is to keep His word: our part is to believe He will keep His word.

We must restore our faith in Gods ability to mean what He says. And do what He says.

When Jesus called his disciples he said, "Follow me and I will make you fishers of men." When Jesus first met his disciples they seemed to be moderately successful in life.

But they were going on a journey that would lead them through the valley of failure and rejection and fear. They had to leave their business and or employment. Their family life was interrupted. Their living arrangements became very insecure. They had to remember that Jesus said he would make them fishers of men – implying that they would ultimately be very successful.

On the day of Pentecost when Peter stood up and preached his sermon, he entered into a realm or zone of success that he could never have imagined. All because he believed that what Jesus had said would happen.

One of our pastor's favourite true stories is about a man in North Queensland who went to the wrong funeral service. There weren't many people there and everyone had to sign a visitor's book. By the time he realized he was at the wrong funeral it was too late to move. He had to sit there until an opportunity came to leave politely.

A month later he received a letter in the mail with a cheque in it. The lady who had died had asked in her will for her estate to be divided up equally among the people who had turned out for her funeral. Everyone knew that this man didn't deserve any money. But the lawyer who was in charge of her estate had to do exactly what she had requested. What she said would happen. What she said was fulfilled.

These days it is easy to get motivated. You listen to someone's story about conquering under great stress and we are encouraged. You listen to a motivational speaker and you get excited. It is easier to get motivated than it is to stay motivated. A speech can get you motivated. A thought can keep you motivated. Here is a thought that should be sown into the deepest part of our heart.

What God says will happen. Believe it!

In the gospel of John chapter 6, we see Jesus feeding the people by a miracle. After the people had enough to eat, Jesus told the disciples to gather the pieces left over. "Let nothing be wasted," said Jesus.

Sometimes we believe that things have been a waste of time; that we have wasted our opportunities. Our God is able to pick up the pieces and get us ready for another day, another opportunity.

Doors can open miraculously in front of us. Don't believe it's been a waste of time and effort. If Jesus cares about bits of food left on the ground how much more does he care about us? If he said let nothing be wasted in that situation, how much more does he say it in our situation.

"Let nothing be wasted."

Believe that what God says will happen.

Chapter 27

April 2013

I have just had a melt-down; it's all taking too long. I have been doing this for two years and the results are disappointing. That's what happens when you have high expectations. Does this happen to people doing a three year university course?

Do they hit the wall after two years? I am still not transformed and my circumstances are only slightly changed.
How can I encourage other people to spend time reading the Bible if the results are so small? When Cain brought his offering to God, he didn't get the result he wanted. But when Abel brought his offering, he received God's favour. So Cain was very angry and his face downcast.

Most people say that Cain was relying on his own self-effort, while Abel was relying on an offering that involved shedding the blood of an animal. Even if you are meditating on the word day and night; you have to make sure you're not trusting in your own efforts.
The whole basis of the new agreement is what Jesus did, not what we do.

When God rescued the Israelites out of Egypt he told them to sacrifice a Passover lamb and put the blood over the doors of their houses.

He would see the blood and not permit the destroyer to enter their houses and strike them down.

When Satan told God, that Job was only obeying Him because there was a hedge of protection around Job, his family and his property, God allowed Satan to attack Job's children and his possessions and finally his health.

Job had been relying on animal sacrifice because he was worried that his children had sinned and cursed God in their hearts. The great news is we don't rely on animal blood for our deliverance and our protection.
We rely on the blood of the Lord Jesus Christ.

Because we are bought back from sin and death by his blood we have become God's possession. We are under the protection of the blood of God's son. The enemy has no permission to enter our lives to kill, steal or destroy.

Satan has to pass over us. We overcome the devil by the blood of the lamb. This is all about what

Jesus has done on the cross. It is not about how much time I have spent reading the Bible.

There is a huge shift of faith going on. If you trust in your own efforts you have to trust in them completely. If you trust in the blood of the new agreement you have to trust in it completely.

I am writing this on Sunday the 21st of April. I have been to the 7.30am communion service at the Anglican Cathedral in Brisbane city. I have not been to a church service in a cathedral since I was a young boy. The service was one hour, there were not many people.

I enjoyed being somewhere different.

They take communion with a big silver cup, not little plastic cups. It's real wine not grape juice. The bread is broken from one large round wafer.

There is a pipe organ filling the building with sound.
There were no jokes, no laughing, everyone was sincere and serious.

I went to the Cathedral to go to a communion service because I had been following up on the theme of the blood of Christ. It was a different perspective and a very different atmosphere.

I enjoyed the service and might do it again.

Chapter 28

May 2013

I'm doing a lot better in May than I was in April. It's not easy realizing that all your self- effort can amount to nothing. We want to get to heaven but heaven wants to manifest down here, in our daily lives. Hence the prayer, "Let it be done on earth as it is in heaven."

When Jesus died on the cross the curtain in the temple was torn in two from top to bottom. Did you hear that? From top to bottom! Not the other way round. If you get it the wrong way round, you will drown in your own good deeds.

Heaven has come to us, God manifests in our lives. If there is now no longer any blockage between heaven and you, will not provision from heaven flow into your situation?

We receive the blessing of God because we are his sons and daughters. Everything we receive is by inheritance; because of who you are and whose you are. Not what you do, except to believe and not doubt. Believe you are God's son or daughter; believe that everything that was separating you from the help of heaven has been removed because of the cross of Christ and the shedding of His blood.

If there is no barrier between you and God in heaven, then we can believe for help and provision to arrive in our lives and the lives of our families. Jesus said we would see heaven open and angels ascending and descending.

When the women visited the tomb they found the stone was rolled away. Who did that? It was the angels. Heaven was already helping out.

Then the women had a conversation with the angels at the tomb. These women received assistance and instruction.

When the disciples realized that Jesus had been raised from the dead they went out into all world and preached the gospel. The Bible tells us that God worked with them and confirmed the Word. When God works with you everything you do succeeds.

That is the message I am getting from reading the New Testament.

All blockages between heaven and me have been removed. I don't have to go to heaven to get what I need; heaven will come to me with provision and assistance. Is there distance between us and God? Is there sin slowing things down? Are our mistakes stopping things from working?

No, the cross and the blood of Jesus took care of all these problems. The help of heaven is here right now. Expect assistance, expect help, if heaven is helping; everything you do will start working.

Your health will start improving, your finances will succeed, and your relationships will prosper. The Lord will surround you with favour as with a shield.

Chapter 29

June 2013

When our family give each other birthday cards we sometimes put some money in the card. When the card is opened the money falls out and the person receiving the card gets very happy. At other times the card contains only words.

Words provide encouragement but actions are even more encouraging. The Bible tells us not to say "be warm and well fed" unless we are going to provide food and clothing.

About a year ago my daughter showed me how to send an email and include an attachment. This was very helpful because I run my own business. Before I knew how to do this I would have to put my invoices in a letter and post them to my customers. Now I can also send photos with my emails to family members.

Before this my emails were just words; now they often contain an attachment.

This makes me a man of action not just words. God tells us not to love in words only but also in deeds. Last week I was talking to a pastor and his wife about their ministry in northern India. They work among the poor and homeless.

The very next day the pastor was hit by a truck while he was riding on his motorbike. He had serious head and leg injuries. The hospital would not operate on him until a financial deposit was made.

Up to this time the pastor and his wife were always requesting prayer, now they needed an action. There comes a time in everyone's life where words and prayer and even prophecy are not meeting the need of the person. Now it is time for words to have something attached to them.

If someone tells you that the Lord is going to meet your needs, let there be enough faith to see something happen in the now, not in the future.

When Jesus said, "This cup is the new covenant in my blood, which is poured out for you," He said the words, but they were not just words because there was an action contained in them. His blood was going to be poured out.

This was a real pouring out. Jesus was subjected to all sorts of actions that caused his blood to flow.

Finally he was hung on a cross, and then one of the soldiers pierced Jesus side with a spear, bringing a sudden flow of blood and water.

Here is an important scripture.

1 Peter 1:18-19
You were redeemed from the empty way of life handed down to you from your ancestors, with the precious blood of Christ, a lamb without blemish or defect.

This is a scripture with an attachment. Normally we might read this and think it is a wonderful thought.

But now we have to read it and have faith to expect it to come to pass in our circumstances. If we are set free from an empty way of life then our lives should immediately reflect that. Fullness should appear that is supernatural.

If God is sending you emails in the form of words of encouragement; will he not send an attachment with the encouragement [email]?

If Gods says he will open the windows of heaven and pour out a blessing so that you will not be able to contain it; we have to believe for that to happen as soon as God says it. Not three months later or three years later.

Now, today, immediately. When did Jesus tell people to come back tomorrow? He did not say, I will go to the cross next year or next week. After he said, "this is the new agreement in my blood," he went out as usual to the Mount of Olives, and his disciples followed him.

He entered into the process of bringing his words to pass. He backed up his words with actions. Jesus emptied himself out on the cross so that we might have his fullness in every area of our lives.

Fullness in our health, finances, relationships, and our purpose in life. "The fullness of him who fills everything in every way."

The centurion replied, "Lord, I do not deserve to have you come under my roof. But just say the word, and my servant will be healed."

This man expected a healing to be attached to the words of Jesus. He did not hope for some comforting words that contained good intentions. He wanted a healing and he knew the words of Jesus were not empty words. By Jesus shedding his blood on the cross; he set an example of words and action.

The centurion believed this and had faith for his email from Jesus to contain an attachment. In that attachment was his servants healing miracle.

We also can expect that we have been set free from a Christian life of empty words into a Christian experience of not just believing but also receiving.

That would make us people of great faith. God will be pleased!

Chapter 30

July 2013

Last September and October we spent a lot of time praying in the Holy Spirit. From then until January everything we did worked well. At the end of January our websites slowed down, the business phone stopped ringing and some ministry opportunities dried up.

Lorna and I realized that we had stopped praying and maybe we should start praying again and this time not stop.

We read a scripture in James 5:18 that we liked a lot.
Again he prayed, and the heavens gave rain, and the earth produced its crops.

We started praying again in May and continued in June. By July we noticed everything began to work. The business phone began to ring, our websites came to life; and ministry doors opened.

The strange thing is; that all through this period I was reading the Bible consistently, day after day, week after week. Why didn't my Bible reading do the job? Is prayer really that important? Does it provide a stairway to Heaven?

Do angels get released to ascend and descend from the throne of God? Here are a couple of scriptures that seem to indicate how prayer works.

Acts 10:3-4
He distinctly saw an angel of God, who came to him and said, "Your prayers have come up before God."

Daniel 10:12
The angel said, "Do not be afraid, Daniel. On the first day your words were heard, and I have come in response to them."

Revelation 8:3-4
The smoke of the incense, together with the prayers of God's people, went up before God from the angel's hand.

What interesting scriptures. Are our prayers really that powerful?

Chapter 31

When a skilful ice-skater starts to spin on the ice they spread their arms out wide. They look great; spinning and turning. Then they bring their arms in close to their body and they increase their speed and turn even faster.

Sometimes we need to focus our attention and concentrate our energy to cut through. The Bible tells us a story about four men who carried their sick friend to a healing meeting where Jesus was ministering. They had to dig through the roof and lower him into the meeting.

This concentration of effort got the attention of Jesus, who then healed this man so he could walk again. When everyone saw their faith, he received his miracle of healing.

Lorna and I live on a small property just outside of Brisbane. We have a lot of trees that drop their branches during our storm season. One particular year I gathered all these branches so they could be burnt. But it rained a lot, so the wood was very wet. I put petrol over a large area of the wood pile.

When I lit the match and threw it in; the petrol exploded but the branches would not burn. I had to get some car oil and build a little fire at one end of the pile. Then I had to get that small area of fire hot enough to be able to burn wet wood. Eventually the fire took hold.

Even though it started to rain the whole pile burnt to the ground. I had wet wood and rain to contend with and still succeeded.

Lorna and I have learnt this lesson. When you are surrounded by unbelief and doubt you have to concentrate all your efforts on a smaller target so you can get a brighter flame. It is nearly 3 years since we dedicated our energy into reading the Bible.

It was so slow at the beginning and the results were disappointing. We kept motivating ourselves by remembering what happened when we did a similar thing earlier in our Christian walk. At that time we spoke our favourite scriptures out loud for a long period of time.

I said to Lorna that the results were a bit slow but I had been reading an interesting scripture in my daily devotions.

1 Corinthians 9:11

If we have sown spiritual seed, is it too much if we reap a material harvest?

The very next day we received a large cheque in the mail from our family lawyer that was totally unexpected. This cheque enabled us to get out of a rental property and into our own home.

Years before we did own our own home, but we sold it to go and help plant a church. We had rented ever since. The day that the cheque came in was the beginning of a season of financial blessing.

Now we read the Bible with faith in our hearts. Often your mind will say, "I did not get anything out of the word today."

Do not listen to your mind; your spirit is getting fed whether your mind thinks so or not. You may go to a restaurant and eat a steak but not enjoy the meal because the steak was cold or tough. Your mind may complain all the way home.

Guess what? While your mind is being negative your stomach is happily digesting that steak so you will have enough physical strength to enjoy your work the next day.

When you read the Bible it is spiritual meat for your spirit. Your spirit is happily digesting the word for spiritual strength to enable you to be strong in faith at your workplace.

This week the beginning of a financial harvest started again, with unexpected money coming in from unusual sources. It all seems too good to be true! Do we really reap a material harvest if we sow spiritual seed?

Please let me know what you think? Do you also have a testimony of Gods financial restoration?

Chapter 32

January 2014

My goal and vision for the last three years was to learn how to turn my believing switch on and keep it on.
It sounds easy to do and it is easy to do if everything around you is going well.

But it is near impossible to do when you are going through a storm. Here are the lessons I have learned.

Believe that reading the Bible creates faith.
Believe that reading and speaking the Bible releases that faith.

I have taken three years to work through all my doubts.
Now I know this is the truth.
When you believe something with all your heart, you enter a place of rest.

Then you are rich in faith.

The End.

A Year Later

I did complete my 3 years of Bible reading. I am writing these words about a year after finishing my experiment.

Yes, I am a changed man. My family will vouch for that. When I started my experiment, I was 55 years old and now I am 59.

I noticed that many Christians around my age were slowly going backwards in their faith, just like I was. I needed to take action!

One of the interesting results was an increase in creativity. I had never written a book before. Now I have written 7 books.

I miss the vision and anticipation that my experiment brought into my life. It was hard to keep going at times, but I could feel the grace of God helping me. I miss that grace.

At the moment I am thinking of doing another three years. I have not told my family yet. I do not want to stop changing for the better.

For some people who have the time and the motivation I would recommend you consider trying something similar.

For others, I am sure that God has the right idea.

Why don't you ask him?

Thanks for reading.

Tony Egar.

Our New Routine.

Lorna and I have a different routine now for building up our faith.

We read the following books out loud on a daily basis.

Galatians.

Ephesians.

Philippians.

Colossians.

Thank you for taking the time to read our story.

If you would like to share with us; please go to our website and leave a message. God Bless from Tony and Lorna

www.tonyegar.com

If you have time to write a review, that would be great!

Made in United States
North Haven, CT
26 April 2022

18564131R00104